Bulletin No. 248

Series F, Geography, 44

DEPARTMENT OF THE INTERIOR

UNITED STATES GEOLOGICAL SURVEY

CHARLES D. WALCOTT, Director

A

GAZETTEER OF INDIAN TERRITORY

BY

HENRY GANNETT

WASHINGTON

GOVERNMENT PRINTING OFFICE

1905

Notice

In many older books, foxing (or discoloration) occurs and, in some instances, print lightens with wear and age. Reprinted books, such as this, often duplicate these flaws, notwithstanding efforts to reduce or eliminate them. The pages of this reprint have been digitally enhanced and, where possible, the flaws eliminated in order to provide clarity of content and a pleasant reading experience.

Originally published
Washington D. C.
1905

Reprinted by:

Janaway Publishing, Inc.
732 Kelsey Ct.
Santa Maria, California 93454
(805) 925-1038
www.janawaygenealogy.com

2006, 2014

ISBN: 978-1-59641-013-8

LETTER OF TRANSMITTAL.

DEPARTMENT OF THE INTERIOR,
UNITED STATES GEOLOGICAL SURVEY,
Washington, D. C., August 13, 1904.

SIR: I transmit herewith the manuscript for a gazetteer of Indian Territory, prepared in the main from atlas sheets of this Survey, and request that it be published as a bulletin.

Respectfully yours, HENRY GANNETT,
Geographer.

Hon. CHARLES D. WALCOTT,
Director United States Geological Survey.

3

A GAZETTEER OF INDIAN TERRITORY.

By Henry Gannett.

GENERAL DESCRIPTION OF THE TERRITORY.

Indian Territory is situated in the south-central part of the United States, between latitudes 33° 25' and 37° 00' and between longitudes 94° 25' and 98° 00'. It is bounded on the north by Kansas, on the east by Arkansas, on the south by Texas, and on the west by Oklahoma.

The north boundary is the thirty-seventh parallel; the east boundary, commencing on the south at Red River, in approximate longitude 94° 29', follows a meridian north to Arkansas River, and thence runs in a direct line to the southwest corner of Missouri. Thence it follows the west line of Missouri, which is a meridian through the mouth of Kansas River, north to the thirty-seventh parallel. The south boundary is the mid-channel of Red River. The west boundary commences in Red River at its intersection with the ninety-eighth meridian and follows this meridian north to Canadian River, thence southeastward along the mid-channel of Canadian River to a point in approximate longitude 96° 46', where the river intersects the middle line of range 5 east. The line then runs north along the range line to its intersection with the North Fork of Canadian River, which it follows eastward to its intersection with the range line between ranges 6 and 7 east; thence it follows the range line north to its intersection with the township line between townships 19 and 20 north, then eastward along this township line to the ninety-sixth meridian, which it follows north to the thirty-seventh parallel. The area of the Territory is 31,400 square miles.

The surface presents considerable variation of relief, ranging from rugged hills to level or rolling prairie. The northern part, including the western part of what is known as the Cherokee Nation, is almost a rolling prairie. The eastern part of this nation, however, lying north of Arkansas River and east of Neosho River, is hilly and broken, containing a part of the Ozark Plateau, which is deeply dissected with streams flowing in canyons.

5

The region between the Arkansas and the Canadian is mostly a rolling plain. South of the Canadian, in the part of the Territory known as the Choctaw and Chickasaw nations, much of the land is hilly and mountainous, being occupied by the Ozark Hills. These consist mainly of narrow winding ridges, with a general east-west trend, separated by narrow valleys. These hills extend into the Territory from western Arkansas and stretch nearly across it, fading out to the westward in the Chickasaw Nation. North of the Ozark Hills the country slopes to the Arkansas and the Canadian, and south of them to Red River.

The lowest part of the Territory, which is its southeast corner on Red River, is about 300 feet above sea level, while its greatest altitude is approximately 3,000 feet.

The principal rivers of the Territory are the Arkansas, the Canadian, and the Red. The Arkansas crosses it in the northern part, flowing in a southeasterly direction. From the north it receives three large branches, the Verdigris, the Neosho, and the Illinois, and from the south the Canadian. Red River forms the southern boundary and receives in its course along the border the waters of Mud Creek, Washita and Blue rivers, Boggy Creek, and Kiamichi River. Little River joins Red River outside the Territory in Arkansas, and drains a considerable area in the southeastern part of the Territory.

About 62 per cent of the area of the Territory is wooded. The chief wooded areas, which lie in the east and the southeast, consist of the Ozark Plateau in eastern Cherokee Nation and the Ozark Hills, mostly in Choctaw Nation. Besides these areas, timber is found more or less scattered in all parts of the Territory. The timber is of great variety; the mountain forests in the eastern and southeastern parts contain considerable amounts of pine, mixed with hard woods; elsewhere the forests are everywhere composed of hard woods, comprising oaks, black walnut, ash, pecan, cottonwood, sycamore, elm, hackberry, maple, and many other species.

The climate of Indian Territory is that of the transition region between the forested lands of the Mississippi Valley and the Great Plains. It is that of the prairie region. The mean annual temperature of much the larger part of the Territory ranges between 60° and 65° F.; but in the northern part, including most of the Cherokee country, and in the mountains of the southeast, in the Choctaw Nation, the mean annual temperature is somewhat lower, ranging from 55° to 60°.

The distribution of mean annual rainfall follows meridians rather than parallels. The eastern part of the Territory is abundantly watered, receiving from 40 to 50 inches annually. The western part of the Territory is not so well watered, but still receives a sufficient amount for all agricultural requirements, the precipitation being from 30 to 40 inches annually.

Almost the entire area of Indian Territory is floored with Carbon-iferous rocks; only in the southern part of the Territory, along Red River, is any considerable area in other formations found. Here there is a belt of Cretaceous beds extending over from central Texas, over-lain in a small area in the southeast corner by Tertiary rocks.

The western part of the Chickasaw Nation, in the southwestern part of the Territory, contains an area of Juratrias rocks. In the eastern part of this nation is a small area of igneous rocks, whose eruption has brought to the surface Silurian beds, extending northwestward across the Carboniferous and Juratrias belts into Oklahoma. It is probably a continuation of the uplift which forms the Wichita Mountains in southeastern Oklahoma.

At various places in the Choctaw Nation coal has been discovered and is being mined in large quantities. The most important of these localities are just east of McAlester and in the vicinity of Coalgate. It is an excellent bituminous coal of Carboniferous age. In the year 1902 there were mined 2,518,452 tons.

The great body of the Territory is divided among five tribes—the Cherokee, whose reservation is in the northern part; the Creek, in the central part; the Seminole, just west of them; the Choctaw, in the southeast; and the Chickasaw, in the southwest. Besides these there are a number of small tribes who have reservations grouped in the northeast corner of the Territory. These are: Quapaw, Peo-ria, Modoc, Ottawa, Wyandot, and Shawnee. The Cherokee, Creek, Choctaw, and Chickasaw were removed from the South to this Terri-tory about 1833. The Seminole, who came from Florida, were, after a costly war, removed to their present reservation in 1845. On these reservations the people have developed a considerable degree of civilization and have been long known as the Five Civilized Tribes. Each tribe has its own system of government, which is patterned in many ways after our State governments, with a governor, a legis-lature, and judiciary of their own. The lands were until recently held in common and occupation gave all the title that was needed. There was an abundance of good land for all and no occasion for the clashing of interests. This condition of things naturally aroused the cupidity of the white man, and many white men settled in the Terri-tory, marrying Indian wives and thereby acquiring tribal rights. By this means squaw-men had acquired much of the valuable coal lands, timber lands, and farm lands. Others followed in their wake. Some white men were suffered to remain in the Territory on condition of paying annual taxes to the tribal government, while a legion of others came and settled without permission, knowing that it would be impos-sible to oust them. These are known as intruders. In 1900 the census showed that the whites in Indian Territory outnumbered the Indians many times over, making a situation fraught with great peril for the

Indians, for it was not to be supposed that the whites would long remain in such overwhelming numbers without title to the lands which they were occupying and subject to Indian laws. This situation had been understood for some time, and the lands have been subdivided into townships and sections preparatory to allotting them to the Indians in severalty and the breaking up of the tribal governments. The allotment has been completed and it is probable that a Territorial form of government will be substituted in the near future for the Indian governments.

The total population of the Territory in 1900 was 392,060, of which not less than 302,680 were whites, 52,500 were Indians, and 36,853 were negroes, either former slaves of the Indians or their descendants.

The following table shows the number of whites, Indians, and negroes in each of the nations and reservations:

Population of Indian Territory by census of 1900.

	White.	Indian.	Negro.
Cherokee Nation	66,951	25,639	9,162
Chickasaw Nation	124,306	5,872	9,066
Choctaw Nation	79,332	10,321	10,123
Creek Nation	25,187	7,963	7,520
Seminole	1,143	1,662	981
Modoc Reservation	96	44	....
Ottawa Reservation	2,029	176	....
Peoria Reservation	995	184	....
Seneca Reservation	799	171	....
Shawnee Reservation	239	58	....
Wyandot Reservation	992	221	....
Quapaw	611	189	....

Population of principal towns in 1900.

Ardmore	5,681
Muscogee	4,254
South McAlester	3,479
Chickasha	3,209
Durant	2,969

During the four years since the census was completed a number of railroads have been built, and other towns of importance have doubtless sprung up.

Of the total population the males formed 53.3 per cent and the females 46.7 per cent. The population was almost entirely of native origin, the persons born in the United States forming 98.8 per cent and the foreign born 1.2 per cent. The whites constituted 77.2 per cent of the total population, the Indians 13.4 per cent, and the negroes 9.4 per cent.

The chief industries of Indian Territory are farming and cattle raising. The rainfall is ample and the soil rich, and nearly every crop produced within the limits of the United States can be raised in the Territory. The prairies of the Cherokee Nation have been in large part leased to cattlemen and enormous herds range over them.

In 1900 the number of farms in the Territory was 45,505. Of these 35,451 were occupied by white farmers, 5,957 by Indian farmers, and 4,097 by negro farmers. Only 25.1 per cent of these farms were said to be owned by the occupants, by which was meant probably that they were occupied by Indians or squaw-men under communal rights; 19.5 per cent were rented for a money rental, and 55.4 per cent were rented for a share in the products.

The total area included within the farms of the Territory was 7,269,081 acres, of which 3,062,193 acres were improved. Of the entire area of the Territory 15.4 per cent was under cultivation. The average size of the farms was 160 acres, considerably larger than the average in the United States.

The following table itemizes the value of farms:

Value of farms, etc., of Indian Territory in 1900.

Land	$39,188,250
Buildings	7,675,190
Implements and machines	3,838,480
Live stock	41,378,695
Total value	92,080,615
Average value per farm	2,026
Value of products	27,602,002
Average annual value per farm	608

The following table shows the products of Indian Territory in 1899:

Principal farm products of Indian Territory in 1899.

Corn	bushels..	30,709,420
Wheat	do....	2,203,780
Oats	do....	4,423,810
Hay	tons..	400,393
Cotton	bales..	143,608

The following table shows the number of live stock:

Statistics of live stock of Indian Territory in 1900.

	Number.
Neat cattle	1,499,364
Horses	217,699
Mules	56,858
Sheep	17,005
Swine	650,255
Value of animals sold in 1900	$6,415,707

Railroad mileage in recent years has been greatly increased; in 1902 there were 1,800 miles within the Territory.

Manufactures are not extensive; the country is too young and too little developed for this branch of industry to have much importance. In 1900 manufacturing establishments with a product of over $500 each numbered only 789, and the capital employed in them was $2,624,265. There were 1,849 employees and the net product, after deducting the value of the raw material was $3,892,181. The chief industries were cotton ginning, with 187 gins; flour milling, with 61 mills, and lumber making, with 6 sawmills.

The entire Territory, with the exception of the small reservations in the northeast corner, has been surveyed and mapped on the scale of 1: 125,000 by the United States Geological Survey in connection with the subdivision of the lands, which was executed by that organization.

The names appearing on the right in the following gazetteer refer to the atlas sheets published separately by the United States Geological Survey.

GAZETTEER.

Abbott; village in Choctaw Nation on St. Louis and San Francisco Railroad.. Antlers.

Abner; post village in Chickasaw Nation.

Academy; post village in Choctaw Nation.

Ada; post village in Chickasaw Nation on St. Louis and San Francisco Railroad .... Stonewall.

Adair; ferry across Neosho River in Cherokee Nation .... Pryor.

Adair; post village in Cherokee Nation on Missouri, Kansas and Texas Railway; population, 268 in 1900; altitude, 681 feet .... Pryor.

Adams; creek in Creek Nation, a right-hand branch of Verdigris River.. Claremore.

Adams; ford across Neosho River in Cherokee Nation........ Pryor.

Adams; post village in Chickasaw Nation.

Addington; post village in Chickasaw Nation on Chicago, Rock Island and Pacific Railway .... Addington.

Adelia; post village in Chickasaw Nation.

Afton; post village in Cherokee Nation on St. Louis and San Francisco Railroad; population, 606 in 1900; altitude, 783 feet .... Wyandotte.

Agatha; post village in Choctaw Nation.

Ague; station on Choctaw, Oklahoma and Gulf Railroad.

Akins; post village in Cherokee Nation .... Tahlequah.

Alabama; creek in Creek Nation, a left-hand branch of North Fork Canadian River .... Wewoka.

Alabama; station on St. Louis and San Francisco Railroad.

Albany; post village in Choctaw Nation .... Bonham.

Alberta; creek in Chickasaw Nation, a right-hand branch of Washita River .... Denison.

Alberty Mountain; summit in Cherokee Nation............. Tahlequah.

Albia; post village in Cherokee Nation on the St. Louis and San Francisco Railroad; altitude, 712 feet................. Vinita.

Albion; post village in Choctaw Nation on St. Louis and San Francisco Railroad; altitude, 655 feet .... Tahlequah.

Alderson; post village in Choctaw Nation on Choctaw, Oklahoma and Gulf Railroad; altitude, 681 feet............... McAlester.

Alex; post village in Chickasaw Nation on Chicago, Rock Island and Pacific Railway.................................. Rush Springs.

Alexanders; station on St. Louis, Iron Mountain and Southern Railway.

Aligan; post village in Cherokee Nation.

Alikchi; post village in Choctaw Nation...................... Alikchi.

Allen; post village in Choctaw Nation....................... Coalgate.

11

Allie; station on St. Louis and San Francisco Railroad.

Alluwe; post village in Cherokee Nation .... Nowata.

Alma; post village in Chickasaw Nation .... Addington.

Amabala; post village in Creek Nation.

Amber; station on St. Louis and San Francisco Railroad.

America; post village in Choctaw Nation.

Amos; post village in Chickasaw Nation.

Amy; post village in Choctaw Nation.

Anadarche; creek in Chickasaw Nation, a left-hand branch of
Hickory Creek, a tributary to Red River heading in West
Fork .... Ardmore.

Anderson; creek in Choctaw Nation, a left-hand branch of
Kiamichi River .... Tuskahoma.

Antioch; post village in Chickasaw Nation .... Pauls Valley.

Antlers; post village in Choctaw Nation on St. Louis and San
Francisco Railroad; elevation, 500 feet.................... Antlers.

Ara; post village in Chickasaw Nation.

Arbeca; creek in Choctaw Nation, a right-hand branch of
Canadian River .... Coalgate.

Arbeka; post village in Creek Nation .... Wewoka.

Arbuckle Mountains; range in Chickasaw Nation .... {Ardmore. / Pauls Valley.

Archibald; post village in Choctaw Nation.

Ardmore; post village in Chickasaw Nation on Gulf, Colorado
and Santa Fe, St. Louis and San Francisco, and Choctaw,
Oklahoma and Gulf railroads; population, 5,681; altitude,
870 feet.. Ardmore.

Ark; post village in Chickasaw Nation .... Gainesville.

Arkansas; river of Colorado, Kansas, Oklahoma Territory,
Indian Territory, and Arkansas; one of the main western
branches of the Mississippi River which it joins on the east
boundary of Arkansas. The river heads in Tennessee Pass
in central Colorado at an altitude of 10,000 feet above the
sea. It flows first south and then east, passing out of the
mountains just west of Canyon City, Colo. Its course is east
across the plains through eastern Colorado and Kansas   Claremore.
changing to southeast shortly before entering Oklahoma   Sallisaw.
Territory, and so continuing through that Territory, Indian Muscogee.
Territory, and Arkansas. Although its total length is 1,497 Okmulgee.
miles, with a drainage area of 185,671 square miles, it car- Sanbois.
ries little water above Little Rock, Ark., except during
times of flood, owing to the fact that the larger part of its
drainage basin is within the arid region. Indeed, in southern Kansas it frequently runs dry in the late summer. It
has many long tributaries, including White, Neosho, Verdigris, Cimarron, and Canadian rivers, but none except the
White brings to it much water.

Armstrong; post village in Choctaw Nation on Missouri, Kansas and Texas Railway; altitude, 569 feet .... Atoka.

Arpelar; post village in Choctaw Nation.

Arthur; post village in Chickasaw Nation .... Addington.

Ash; creek in Choctaw Nation, a left-hand branch of Gaines {Tuskahoma / McAlester. / Canadian.
Creek, a tributary to Canadian River.

Ash; creek in Creek Nation, a right-hand branch of Arkansas River... Okmulgee.

Ashby; station on St. Louis, Iron Mountain and Southern Railway.

Ashland; post village in Choctaw Nation.

Atlas; post village in Choctaw Nation.

Atlee; post village in Chickasaw Nation...................... Addington.

Atoka; post village in Choctaw Nation on Missouri, Kansas and Texas Railway; altitude, 558 feet......................... Atoka.

Austin; village in Cherokee Nation.......................... Nowata.

Aylesworth; post village in Chickasaw Nation on St. Louis and San Francisco Railroad.

Bache; post village in Choctaw Nation on Choctaw, Oklahoma and Gulf Railroad.

Bachelor; creek in Creek Nation, a left-hand branch of Deep Fork of Canadian River.. Nuyaka.

Backbone Mountains; range in Choctaw Nation, extending into Arkansas... Sallisaw.

Bacone; post village in Creek Nation on Missouri, Kansas and Texas Railway... Muscogee.

Bad; creek in Creek Nation, a left-hand branch of North Fork of Canadian River.. Wewoka.

Bailey; post village in Chickasaw Nation..................... Rush Springs.

Baird; village in Choctaw Nation........................... Winding Stair.

Bald Mountain; summit in Creek Nation..................... Wewoka.

Baldhill; post village in Creek Nation.

Ballara; station on the Kansas City Southern Railway.

Ballard; creek in Cherokee Nation, a left-hand branch of Illinois River. ⎰Siloam Springs. ⎱Tahlequah.

Ballard; post village in Chickasaw Nation.................... Siloam Springs.

Banger; creek in Cherokee Nation, a left-hand branch of Neosho River... Muscogee.

Bannett; station in Choctaw Nation on Choctaw, Oklahoma and Gulf Railroad... McAlester.

Banty; post village in Choctaw Nation.

Baptising; creek in Creek Nation, a right-hand branch of North Fork of Canadian River........................... Canadian.

Baptist; post village in Cherokee Nation on Kansas City Southern Railway... Siloam Springs.

Barnard; post village in Creek Nation.

Barnett; station on Choctaw, Oklahoma and Gulf Railroad.

Baron; post village in Cherokee Nation.

Barren; station in Cherokee Nation on Kansas City Southern Railway... Tahlequah.

Barren Fork; left-hand branch of Illinois River, rising in Arkansas and flowing into the Illinois a few miles south of Tahlequah, Cherokee Nation............................. Tahlequah.

Barren Fork; station on Kansas City Southern Railway.

Bartlesville; post village in Cherokee Nation on Atchison, Topeka and Santa Fe and Missouri, Kansas and Texas railways; population, 698..................................... Nowata.

Battle; creek in Creek Nation, a right-hand branch of Flat Rock Creek, a tributary to North Fork of Canadian River. Wewoka.

Baum; post village in Chickasaw Nation.................... Tishomingo.

Baumgarten Hollow; valley of Baumgarten Creek, a tribu-⌠Tahlequah.
tary to Illinois River, in Cherokee Nation.   ⌡Siloam Springs.
Bayou; creek in Cherokee Nation, a small left-hand branch of
Arkansas River .... Sallisaw.
Bayou Manard; creek in Cherokee Nation, a left-hand branch
of Arkansas River... Muscogee.
Beach; creek in Choctaw Nation, a right-hand branch of Moun-⌠Lukfata.
tain Fork River, a tributary to Little River.   ⌡Winding Stair.
Beach; post village in Choctaw Nation.
Bear; creek in Cherokee Nation, a right-hand branch of Lee
Creek, a tributary to Arkansas River .... Tahlequah.
Bear; creek in Choctaw Nation, a left-hand branch of Moun-
tain Fork River, a tributary to Little River .... Lukfata.
Bear; creek in Choctaw Nation, a left-hand branch of Brazil⌠Sansbois.
Creek, a tributary to Poteau River.   ⟨Sallisaw.
                                           ⌡Winding Stair.
Bearden; post village in Creek Nation .... Wewoka.
Bear Lake; in Chickasaw Nation........................... Bonham.
Beaty; creek in Cherokee Nation, a right-hand branch of
Spavinaw Creek, a tributary to Neosho River .... Siloam Springs.
Beaver; creek in Chickasaw Nation, a left-hand branch of
Red River... Addington.
Beaver; creek in Choctaw Nation, a right-hand branch of
Kiamichi River .... Antlers.
Beaver; creek in Choctaw Nation, a left-hand branch of Sans-
bois Creek .... Tahlequah.
Beaver; creek in Choctaw Nation, a right-hand branch of Cana-
dian River.. Wewoka.
Beaverdam; creek in Choctaw Nation, a left-hand tributary
of Boggy Creek... Antlers.
Beckwith; village in Cherokee Nation..................... Siloam Springs.
Bee; creek in Choctaw Nation, a left-hand tributary to Boggy
Creek.. Antlers.
Bee; post village in Chickasaw Nation.
Beebee; post village in Chickasaw Nation .... Stonewall.
Beef; creek in Chickasaw Nation, a right-hand branch of
Washita River.. Pauls Valley.
Beef Creek; village in Chickasaw Nation................... Pauls Valley.
Beggs; post village in Creek Nation.
Belcher; village in Creek Nation .... Canadian.
Belle Starr; creek in Cherokee Nation, a left-hand branch of
Canadian River .... Sansbois.
Belle Starr Mountain; summit in Choctaw Nation........... McAlester.
Belton; post village in Chickasaw Nation................... Tishomingo.
Bengal; post village in Choctaw Nation on St. Louis and Paris
Line of St. Louis and San Francisco Railroad; altitude, 646
feet .... Tuskahoma.
Benge; post village in Cherokee Nation.
Benkiller's; ferry across Illinois River, a tributary to
Arkansas River, in Cherokee Nation..................... Muscogee.
Ben Knight; creek in Cherokee Nation, a right-hand branch
of Barren Creek, a tributary to Illinois River............. Tahlequah.
Bennett; post village in Cherokee Nation .... Sansbois.

Bennington; post village in Choctaw Nation on St. Louis and
San Francisco Railroad .... Atoka.

Bently; post village in Choctaw Nation.

Berwyn; post village in Chickasaw Nation on Gulf, Colorado
and Santa Fe Railway; population, 276; altitude, 727 feet. Ardmore.

Bethel; post village in Choctaw Nation...................... Lukfata.

Bevan; creek in Cherokee Nation, a right-hand branch of
Caney Creek, a tributary to Verdigris River.............. Claremore.

Big; creek in Cherokee Nation, a left-hand branch of Verdigris ⎰Vinita.
River, a tributary to Arkansas River.   ⎱Nowata.

Big; creek in Chickasaw Nation, a right-hand branch of Canadian River.. Stonewall.

Big; creek in Choctaw Nation, a right-hand branch of Black ⎧Winding Stair.
Fork River, a tributary to Poteau River, heading in ⎨Poteau.
Arkansas.   ⎩Mountain.

Big; creek in Choctaw Nation, a left-hand branch of Mountain
Fork River, a tributary to Little River.................... Lukfata.

Big; creek in Choctaw Nation, a left-hand branch of Kiamichi
River... Winding Stair.

Big; creek in Choctaw Nation, a right-hand branch of Canadian River.. Coalgate.

Big; lake in Cherokee Nation, cut-off from Verdigris River... Claremore.

Big Branch; creek in Choctaw Nation, a right-hand branch of ⎰Sallisaw.
James Fork, a tributary to Poteau River.   ⎱Fort Smith.

Big Cabin; post village in Cherokee Nation on Missouri, Kansas and Texas Railway; elevation, 718 feet................ Vinita.

Big Cedar; post village in Choctaw Nation.

Big Eagle; creek in Choctaw Nation, a right-hand branch of
Eagle Fork, a tributary to Mountain Fork River........... Winding Stair.

Big Hale; creek in Choctaw Nation, a left-hand branch of Kiamichi River... Alikchi.

Big One; creek in Choctaw Nation, a right-hand branch of ⎰Antlers.
Cedar Creek, a tributary to Kiamichi River.   ⎱Alikchi.

Big Sand; creek in Chickasaw Nation, a left-hand branch of
Washita River .... Tishomingo.

Big Sandy; creek in Chickasaw Nation, a right-hand branch ⎰Stonewall.
of Sandy Creek, a tributary to Washita River.   ⎱Pauls Valley.

Big Sandy; creek in Choctaw Nation, a left-hand branch of
Sand Creek, a tributary to Muddy Boggy Creek .... Coalgate.

Big Spring; creek in Chickasaw Nation, a right-hand branch
of Clear Boggy Creek .... Stonewall.

Bills Branch; creek in Chickasaw Nation, a left-hand branch
of Red River.. Gainsville.

Billy; creek in Choctaw Nation, a left-hand branch of Kiamichi
River... Winding Stair

Billy; creek in Creek Nation, a left-hand branch of Verdigris
River... Muscogee.

Birch; creek in Choctaw Nation, a right-hand branch of North
Boggy Creek, a tributary to Muddy Boggy Creek.......... Claremore.

Bird; creek in Cherokee Nation, a right-hand branch of Verdigris River, a tributary to Arkansas River................. Claremore.

Bird; creek in Choctaw Nation, a left-hand branch of Kiamichi ⎰Alikchi.
River.   ⎱Clarkville.

Birds; ferry across Illinois River, a tributary to Arkansas
River, in Cherokee Nation .... Muscogee.

Bitter; creek in Chickasaw Nation, a left-hand branch of
Washita River, heading in East and North forks .... Chickasha.

Bitter; creek in Choctaw Nation, a left-hand branch of Cedar {Antlers.
Creek, a tributary to Kiamichi River.   {Alikchi.

Bitter; creek in Choctaw Nation, a right-hand branch of Clear
Boggy Creek .... Atoka.

Bitter, or Whiskey, Gap; creek in Cherokee Nation, a left-
hand branch of Pryor Creek, a tributary to Neosho River. Pryor.

Bixby; post village in Creek Nation.

Black; creek in Choctaw Nation, a right-hand branch of
Muddy Boggy Creek .... Coalgate.

Black Bear; creek in Chickasaw Nation, a left-hand branch of {Rush Springs.
Wildhorse Creek, a tributary to Washita River.   {Addington.

Blackbird; creek, a right-hand branch of Fourteenmile Creek, {Siloam Springs.
a tributary of Neosho River.   {Pryor.

Black Fork; river in Cherokee Nation, fork of the Skin Bayou
River, tributary to Arkansas River .... Tahlequah.

Black Fork; right-hand branch of Little River in Choctaw
Nation .... Alikchi.

Black Fork; right-hand branch of Poteau River, heading in {Winding Stair.
Arkansas and flowing through Choctaw Nation.   {Poteau Sheet.

Black Fork Mountain; an east and west ridge of the Ozark⎤
Hills, separating Black Fork and Big Creek. It lies mainly |Poteau Sheet.
in Arkansas, but extends into Choctaw Nation; extreme ⎨Winding Stair.
height, 2,650 feet.   ⎦

Blackgum; post village in Cherokee Nation .... Tahlequah.

Blackjack; creek in Cherokee Nation, a right-hand branch
of Caney River, a tributary to Verdigris River............. Claremore.

Blackjack Prairie; level stretch of land between the villages
of Ulm and Kansas, in Cherokee Nation................... Siloam Springs.

Black Knob; ridge in Choctaw Nation .... Atoka.

Blaine; post village in Choctaw Nation...................... Sallisaw.

Blanco; post village in Choctaw Nation.

Blue; creek in Chickasaw Nation, a left-hand branch of Blue
River.. Stonewall.

Blue; post village in Choctaw Nation......................... Bonham.

Blue; river in Choctaw and Chickasaw nations, a left-hand⎧Bonham.
branch of Red River, heading in the northern part of⎨Atoka.
Chickasaw Nation and flowing southeast to its mouth..... |Pauls Valley.
                                                                           |Tishomingo.
                                                                           ⎩Stonewall.

Blue Bouncer; group of hills in Choctaw Nation, south of
Kiamichi River .... Winding Stair.

Blue Bouncer Mountain; part of the Kiamichi Mountains in
Choctaw Nation .... Winding Stair.

Bluejacket; post village in Cherokee Nation on Missouri, Kansas and Texas Railway; population, 303................... Vinita.

Blue Jacket; station on Missouri, Kansas, and Texas Railway; elevation, 774 feet.

Blue Mountain; summit in Choctaw Nation................ Sansbois.

Blue Spring; branch in Cherokee Nation, a left-hand branch
of Flint Creek, a tributary to Illinois River .... Siloam Springs.

Bluff; post village in Choctaw Nation.

Bob; post village in Chickasaw Nation on Gulf, Colorado and Santa Fe Railway .... Gainesville.

Bobtail; creek in Cherokee Nation, a left-hand branch of Bayou Manard.. Muscogee.

Boggs; branch in Cherokee Nation, a left-hand branch of Big Creek, a tributary to Verdigris River .... Vinita.

Boggy; creek in Chickasaw Nation, a left-hand branch of Black Bear Creek, a tributary to Washita River .... Rush Springs.

Boggy; creek in Chickasaw Nation, a left-hand branch of Red River. { Denison. } Tishomingo.

Boggy; creek in Chickasaw Nation, a right-hand branch of Canadian River.. Chickasha.

Boggy; creek, a left-hand branch of Red River, formed by the junction of Clear Boggy Creek and Muddy Boggy Creek, the former of which heads in Chickasaw Nation and the latter in Choctaw Nation. { Paris. } Antlers.

Boggy Depot; post village in Choctaw Nation .... Atoka.

Boiling Spring; creek in Choctaw Nation, a small intermittent left-hand branch of Gaines Creek, a tributary to Canadian River .... Tuskahoma.

Bois d'Arc; creek in Chickasaw Nation, a small intermittent right-hand branch of Clear Boggy Creek.................. Stonewall.

Bois d'Arc; creek in Choctaw Nation, a right-hand branch of Clear Boggy Creek....................................... Atoka.

Bois d'Arc; right-hand branch of Blue River, in Chickasaw and Choctaw nations...................................... Atoka.

Bokchito; creek in Choctaw Nation, a left-hand branch of Boggy Creek .... Antlers.

Bokchito; creek in Choctaw Nation, a left-hand branch of Blue River, a tributary of Red River.................... Atoka.

Bokchito; post village in Choctaw Nation.................... Atoka.

Bokchito; station on St. Louis and San Francisco Railroad.

Bokhoma; post village in Choctaw Nation.

Bokoshe; post village in Choctaw Nation on Fort Smith and Western Railroad; population, 153........................ Sallisaw.

Boktukola; creek in Choctaw Nation, a right-hand branch of Mountain Fork River, a tributary to Little River......... Lukfata.

Boley; post village in Choctaw Nation.

Bomar; station on Gulf, Colorado and Santa Fe Railway; population, 826.

Bond; station in Creek Nation on Missouri, Kansas and Texas Railway .... Canadian.

Bone; creek in Chickasaw Nation, a left-hand branch of Walnut Bayou, a tributary to Red River...................... Gainesville.

Bon Ton; village in Choctaw Nation........................ Clarkesville.

Boswell; post village in Choctaw Nation on St. Louis and San Francisco Railroad.

Boudinot; creek in Cherokee Nation, a left-hand branch of Arkansas River .... Muscogee.

Boudinot; station on the Gulf, Colorado and Santa Fe Railway.

Bounds; ferry across Red River in Chickasaw Nation .... Denison.

Bower; post village in Choctaw Nation...................... Canadian,

Bowles; post village in Chickasaw Nation.

Boynton; post village in Creek Nation on St. Louis and San
Francisco Railroad.

Braden; post village in Choctaw Nation on Kansas City
Southern Railway ------------------------------------- Sallisaw.

Bradley; post village in Chickasaw Nation on Chicago, Rock
Island and Pacific Railway------------------------- Rush Springs.

Brady; post village in Chickasaw Nation ------------------- Pauls Valley.

Braggs; post village in Cherokee Nation on Arkansas Valley
Division of St. Louis, Iron Mountain and Southern Railway. Muscogee.

Brazil; creek in Choctaw Nation, a left-hand branch of Poteau { Sallisaw.
River. { Tuskahoma.

Brazil; post village in Choctaw Nation------------------- Sallisaw.

Brent; post village in Cherokee Nation------------------- Sallisaw.

Briartown; post village in Cherokee Nation---------------- Sansbois.

Bridge; creek in Chickasaw Nation, a right-hand branch of
Walnut Creek, a tributary to Canadian River ----------:. Chickasha.

Brier; creek in Chickasaw Nation, a left-hand branch of Red { Denison.
River. { Tishomingo.

Brier; creek in Choctaw Nation, a left-hand branch of Caddo
Creek, a tributary to Blue River---------------------- Atoka.

Brier; creek in Choctaw Nation, a right-hand branch of Muddy
Boggy Creek --- Atoka.

Brier; creek in Choctaw Nation, a very small right-hand
branch of Arkansas River-------------------------- Sansbois.

Brier; creek in Creek Nation, a right-hand branch of Nuyaka
Creek, a tributary to Deep Fork of Canadian River ------- Nuyaka.

Bristow; post village in Creek Nation on St. Louis and San
Francisco Railroad; population, 626 ------------------- Nuyaka.

Brock; post village in Chickasaw Nation ------------------- Ardmore.

Broken Arrow; creek in Creek Nation, a left-hand branch of
Arkansas River ------------------------------------- Okmulgee.

Broken Arrow; post village in Creek Nation.

Brooken; creek in Choctaw Nation, a small right-hand branch
of Canadian River---------------------------------- Sansbois.

Brooken; village in Choctaw Nation ---------------------- Sansbois.

Brown; station on St. Louis and San Francisco Railroad.

Browns; creek in Creek Nation, a left-hand branch of Little
Deep Fork Creek, tributary to Deep Fork of Canadian
River-- Nuyaka.

Browns; creek in Creek Nation, a right-hand branch of Little
Polecat Creek, a tributary through Polecat River to Arkansas River --- Nuyaka.

Browns; ferry across Red River in Chickasaw Nation -------- Ardmore.

Browns; fork in Seminole Nation, a right-hand branch of
Fishing Creek, a tributary to North Fork of Canadian
River-- Seminole.

Brownsville; post village in Chickasaw Nation------------- Denison.

Brush; creek in Cherokee Nation, a right-hand branch of Big
Creek, a tributary to Verdigris River ------------------ Vinita.

Brush; creek in Cherokee Nation, a right-hand branch of
Spavinaw Creek, a tributary to Neosho River ----------- Siloam Springs.

Brush; creek in Cherokee Nation, a left-hand branch of Little
Caney Creek, a tributary to Caney River -------------- Nowata.

Brush; creek in Creek and Cherokee nations, a right-hand
   branch of Neosho River ------------------------------ Pryor.
Brush Hill; post village in Creek Nation------------------ Canadian.
Brushyhead; post village in Cherokee Nation.
Brushy; creek in Cherokee Nation, a left-hand branch of Salli-
   saw Creek, a tributary to Arkansas River -------------- Tahlequah.
Brushy; creek in Chickasaw Nation, a right-hand branch of
   Red River -- Tishomingo.
Brushy; creek in Choctaw Nation, a left-hand branch of
   Gaines Creek, a tributary to Canadian River ----------- McAlester.
Brushy; post village in Cherokee Nation.
Brushy Mountain; summit in Cherokee Nation ----------- Sallisaw.
Bryant; station on St. Louis and San Francisco Railroad.
Bryant Hollow; valley of Bryant Creek, a right-hand branch
   of Spring Creek, a tributary to Neosho River in Cherokee
   Nation--------------:------------------------------- Pryor.
Buck; creek, a left-hand branch of Caney River, a tributary to⎰Claremore.
   Verdigris River.   ⎱Nowata.
Buck; creek in Chickasaw Nation, a left-hand branch of Clear⎰Stonewall.
   Boggy Creek.   ⎱Coalgate.
Buck; creek in Choctaw Nation, a right-hand branch of Clear
   Boggy Creek --- Atoka.
Buck; creek in Choctaw Nation, a left-hand branch of Little
   River--- Shawneetown.
Buck; creek in Choctaw Nation, a right-hand branch of Kia-⎰Antlers.
   michi River.   ⎱McAlester.
Buck; creek in Choctaw Nation, a left-hand branch of Brazil
   Creek, a tributary to Poteau River------------------- Sallisaw.
Buck; post village in Choctaw Nation.
Buck; station on Missouri, Kansas and Texas Railway.
Buck Creek; small village in Choctaw Nation ------------- Sallisaw.
Buckeye; creek in Creek Nation, a right-hand branch of⎰Wewoka.
   Deep Fork Canadian River.   ⎱Nuyaka.
Buckhorn; creek in Chickasaw Nation, a left-hand tributary
   to Red River-- Rush Springs.
Buckhorn; creek in Chickasaw Nation, a left-hand branch⎰Ardmore.
   of Rock Creek, a tributary to Washita River.   ⎱Tishomingo.
Buckhorn; creek in Choctaw Nation, a right-hand branch,⎰McAlester.
   through Wildhorse Creek, of Caney Creek.   ⎱Coalgate.
Buckhorn; post village in Chickasaw Nation -------------- Tishomingo.
Buffalo; creek in Choctaw Nation, a left-hand branch of
   Mountain Fork River, a tributary to Little River which
   rises in Arkansas----------------------------------- Lukfata.
Buffalo; creek in Choctaw Nation, a left-hand branch of Kia-
   michi River--- Tuskahoma.
Buffalo; creek in Choctaw Nation, a left-hand branch of
   Gaines Creek, a tributary to Canadian River ----------- Tuskahoma.
Buffalo; creek in Choctaw Nation, a small right-hand branch
   of Gaines Creek, a tributary to Canadian River---------- Tishomingo.
Buffalo Mountain; short ridge of Ozark Hills in Choctaw
   Nation; maximum altitude, 2,100 feet------------------ Tuskahoma.
Bull; creek in Cherokee Nation, a left-hand branch of Cabin
   Creek, a tributary to Neosho River ------------------- Vinita.

Bull; creek in Chickasaw Nation, a left-hand branch of Walnut
Bayou, a tributary to Red River........................... Ardmore.

Bull; creek in Choctaw Nation, a left-hand branch of Little
River, which rises in Choctaw Nation and flows through
Arkansas into Little River .... Lukfata.

Bull; creek in Choctaw Nation, a left-hand branch of Coal Creek,
a tributary of Canadian River through Gaines Creek...... Canadian.

Bull; creek in Choctaw Nation, a right-hand branch of Gates
Creek, a tributary to Kiamichi River .... Alikchi.

Bull; creek in Creek Nation, a left-hand branch of Verdigris
River.. Pryor.

Bull; station on St. Louis, Iron Mountain and Southern
Railway .... Pryor.

Bunch; post village in Cherokee Nation on Kansas City Southern Railway .... Tahlequah.

Buncombe; creek in Chickasaw Nation, a left-hand branch of {Denison.
Red River.   Tishomingo.

Burgevin; village in Choctaw Nation; elevation, 440 feet .... Sallisaw.

Burney; post village in Creek Nation.

Burneyville; post village in Chickasaw Nation .... Gainesville.

Burris; ferry across Little River in Choctaw Nation.......... Shawneetown.

Burros; creek in Chickasaw Nation, an intermittent left-hand
branch of Sandy Creek, a tributary to Canadian River .... Stonewall.

Burse; post village in Choctaw Nation.

Burt; town in Chickasaw Nation............................. Rush Springs.

Bushyhead; village in Cherokee Nation on St. Louis and San
Francisco Railroad .... Pryor.

Bushyhead Mountain; summit in Cherokee Nation.......... Siloam Springs.

Bushy Mountain; summit in Cherokee Nation............... Sallisaw.

Butcher Pen; creek in Chickasaw Nation, a left-hand branch
of Washita river... Tishomingo.

Butler; creek in Cherokee Nation, a very small right-hand
branch of Caney River, a tributary to Verdigris River..... Nowata.

Butler; creek in Creek Nation, a left-hand branch of Dirty
Creek, a tributary of Arkansas River...................... Muscogee.

Butler; village in Choctaw Nation, on St. Louis and San Francisco Railroad, in valley of Kiamichi River .... Antlers.

Butner; post village in Creek Nation.

Buzzard; creek in Choctaw Nation, a left-hand branch of Red
River.. Clarkesville.

Buzzard; creek in Choctaw Nation, a left-hand branch of {Tuskahoma.
Kiamichi River.   Winding Stair.

Byars; post village in Chickasaw Nation on Gulf, Colorado and
Santa Fe Railway.

Byrne; post village in Choctaw Nation.

Cabanis; post village in Choctaw Nation.

Cabin; creek in Cherokee Nation, a right-hand branch of {Pryor.
Neosho River.   Vinita.

Cache; creek in Choctaw Nation, a right-hand branch of
Arkansas River .... Sallisaw.

Cache; village in Choctaw Nation............................ Sallisaw.

Caddo; creek in Chickasaw Nation, a right-hand branch of {Ardmore.
Washita River.   Tishomingo.
                                                           Addington.

Caddo; creek in Choctaw Nation, a left-hand branch of Blue
River, a tributary to Red River........................... Atoka.
Caddo; post village in Choctaw Nation on Missouri, Kansas
and Texas Railway; elevation, 708 feet.................... Atoka.
Caddo Hills; isolated hills in Choctaw Nation............... Atoka.
Cade; post village in Choctaw Nation.
Cairo; post village in Choctaw Nation on Choctaw, Oklahoma,
and Gulf Railroad.
Cale; station on Missouri, Kansas and Texas Railway.
California; creek in Cherokee Nation, a right-hand branch of
Verdigris River, a tributary to Arkansas River............ Nowata.
Calloway; post village in Choctaw Nation.
Calunchety Hollow; valley of Calunchety Creek, a right-hand
branch of Flint Creek, a tributary to Illinois River, in Cher-
okee Nation .... Siloam Springs.
Calvin; post village in Choctaw Nation on Choctaw, Oklahoma
and Gulf Railroad; elevation, 715 feet..................... Coalgate.
Cameron; post village in Choctaw Nation on Paris Branch of
St. Louis and San Francisco Railroad .... Sallisaw.
Camp; creek in Cherokee Nation, a left-hand branch of Arkan-⎰Fort Smith.
sas River.   ⎱Sallisaw.
Camp; creek in Chickasaw Nation, a right-hand branch of
Washita River .... Tishomingo.
Campbell; post village in Cherokee Nation on Kansas and
Arkansas Valley Division of St. Louis, Iron Mountain and
Southern Railway .... Muscogee.
Canadian; post village in Choctaw Nation on Missouri, Kansas
and Texas Railway; population, 522 .... Canadian.
Canadian; river of New Mexico, Oklahoma, and Indian Territory, a large right-hand branch of Arkansas River which
heads in Raton Pass, in northern New Mexico, and flows at
first south and then east down the slope of the plains, join-
ing Arkansas River in the eastern part of Indian Territory;
length, 758 miles.
Canadian Sandy; creek in Chickasaw Nation, a right-hand
branch of Canadian River................................. Pauls Valley.
Canadian Sandy; creek in Chickasaw Nation, a right-hand
branch of Sandy Creek, a tributary to Canadian River .... Stonewall.
Cane; creek in Choctaw Nation, a right-hand branch of Kiamichi
River.. Antlers.
Cane; creek in Creek Nation, a right-hand branch of Cloud
Creek, a tributary to Arkansas River...................... Okmulgee.
Caney; branch in Chickasaw Nation, a left-hand branch of Rock
Creek, a tributary of Red River .... Denison.
Caney; creek, a left-hand branch of Little River, heading in
Choctaw Nation and flowing into Arkansas................ Shawneetown.
Caney; creek in Cherokee Nation, a left-hand branch of Illinois
River.. Tahlequah.
Caney; creek in Choctaw Nation, a right-hand branch of Clear
Boggy Creek .... Atoka.
Caney; creek in Choctaw Nation, a right-hand branch of Little
River .... Alikchi.
Caney; creek in Choctaw Nation, a right-hand branch of Wild-
horse Creek, a tributary to Gaines Creek.................. McAlester.

Caney; creek in Choctaw Nation, a right-hand branch of Muddy
Boggy Creek .... Coalgate.

Caney; post village in Choctaw Nation on Missouri, Kansas
and Texas Railway; elevation, 532 feet.................... Atoka.

Caney; river in Cherokee Nation, a right-hand branch of Ver-⎱
digris River, a tributary to Arkansas River, heading in Kan-⎰ Claremore.
sas and flowing south.   Nowata.

Caney Boggy; creek in Choctaw Nation, a left-hand branch of
Muddy Boggy Creek....................................... Antlers.

Caney Boggy; creek in Choctaw Nation, a left-hand branch
of Muddy Creek.. Coalgate.

Canyon; creek in Chickasaw Nation, a right-hand branch of
Clear Boggy Creek....................................... Stonewall.

Carbon; post village in Choctaw Nation on Missouri, Kansas
and Texas Railway.

Carr; creek in Creek Nation, a left-hand branch of North Fork
Canadian River, a tributary to Canadian River .... Canadian.

Carson; post village in Creek Nation.

Cartersville; post village in Choctaw Nation .... Sallisaw.

Cass; lake in Cherokee Nation north of Caney River .... Nowata.

Castle; post village in Creek Nation on Fort Smith and Western
Railroad.

Caston; station on St. Louis and San Francisco Railroad.

Cat; creek in Cherokee Nation, a right-hand branch of Neosho
River... Pryor.

Catale; post village in Cherokee Nation on St. Louis and San
Francisco Railroad .... Vinita.

Catfish; creek in Creek Nation, a left-hand branch of Little
Deep Creek, a tributary through Little Deep Fork Creek
to Deep Fork of Canadian River.......................... Nuyaka.

Cathay; post village in Creek Nation.

Catoosa; post village in Cherokee Nation on St. Louis and San
Francisco Railroad; population, 241........................ Claremore.

Cavanal; village in Choctaw Nation on Paris Line of St. Louis
and San Francisco Railroad; elevation, 469 feet........... Winding Stair.

Cavanal Mountain; summit in Choctaw Nation.............. Sallisaw.

Caw; creek in Cherokee Nation, a right-hand branch of Neosho
River... Wyandotte.

Cayuga; post village in Seneca Reservation.................. Wyandotte.

Cedar; post village in Creek Nation.

Cedar; creek in Cherokee Nation, a left-hand branch of Arkansas River... Muscogee.

Cedar; creek in Cherokee Nation, a left-hand branch of Coon
Creek, a tributary to Caney Creek .... Nowata.

Cedar; creek in Cherokee Nation, a small left-hand branch of ⎰Tahlequah.
Little Sallisaw Creek, a tributary to Arkansas River.   ⎱Sallisaw.

Cedar; creek in Cherokee Nation, a left-hand branch of Verdi-⎰Nowata.
gris River, a tributary to Arkansas River.   ⎱Vinita.

Cedar; creek in Chickasaw Nation, a left-hand branch of Pennington Creek, a tributary to Washita River.............. Tishomingo.

Cedar; creek in Choctaw Nation, a left-hand branch of Brazil
Creek, a tributary to Poteau River....................... Sallisaw.

Cedar; creek in Choctaw Nation, a left-hand branch of Glover Creek, a tributary to Little River.......................... Lukfata.

Cedar; creek in Choctaw Nation, a left-hand branch of Kiami-{ Antlers.
chi River, heading in West Fork.   { Alikchi.

Cedar; creek in Choctaw Nation, a right-hand branch of Black Fork, a tributary to Poteau River.......................... Winding Stair.

Cedar; creek in Choctaw Nation, a right-hand branch of Muddy Boggy Creek....................................... Coalgate.

Cedar; creek in Choctaw Nation, a small right-hand branch of Poteau River... Sallisaw.

Cedar; creek in Choctaw Nation, a right-hand branch of James Fork, a tributary to Poteau River.......................... Sallisaw.

Cedar; creek in Choctaw Nation, a left-hand branch of Kiamichi River.. Tuskahoma.

Cedar; creek in Creek Nation, a left-hand branch of Arkansas River.. Okmulgee.

Celestine; post village in Choctaw Nation.

Center; post village in Chickasaw Nation..................... Stonewall.

Centralia; post village in Cherokee Nation.................. Vinita.

Chaffee; post village in Cherokee Nation.

Chagris; post village in Chickasaw Nation .... Addington.

Chance; post village in Cherokee Nation .... Siloam Springs.

Chant; post village in Choctaw Nation.

Chapel; post village in Cherokee Nation.

Charles; lake of crescent shape in Red River bottom land in Choctaw Nation... Shawneetown.

Chase; post village in Creek Nation on St. Louis and San Francisco Railroad.

Checotah; post village in Creek Nation on Missouri, Kansas and Texas Railway; population, 805...................... Canadian.

Cheek; creek in Chickasaw Nation, a left-hand branch of Washita River... Pauls Valley.

Cheek; post village in Chickasaw Nation..................... Ardmore.

Chelsea; post village in Cherokee Nation on St. Louis and San Francisco Railroad; population, 566...................... Vinita.

Cherokee; creek in Cherokee Nation, a left-hand branch of Spavinaw Creek... Siloam Springs.

Cherokee Junction; station on St. Louis, Iron Mountain and Southern Railway.

Cherokee Nation; reservation occupying the northern part of the Territory with an area of 7,861 square miles. West of Neosho River the surface consists mostly of a rolling prairie, but slightly timbered. East of Neosho and Arkansas rivers the Ozark Plateau extends into the Territory from Arkansas, and the country is well timbered nearly down to the rivers. The capital is Tahlequah. Population, white, 66,951; Indian, 25,639; negro, 9,162; total, 101,754.

Cherokee Sandy; creek in Chickasaw Nation, a left-hand branch of Washita River................................. Pauls Valley.

Cherryvale; village in Choctaw Nation on Choctaw, Oklahoma and Gulf Railroad .... McAlester.

Chicago, Rock Island and Pacific Railway; a system with several lines traversing the Territory in various directions.

Chickasaw; creek in Choctaw Nation, a left-hand branch of
Muddy Boggy Creek .... Antlers.

Chickasaw; creek in Choctaw Nation, a small right-hand { Antlers.
branch of Cedar Creek, a tributary to Kiamichi River.   { Atoka.

Chickasaw Nation; reservation in the southwestern part of
the Territory with an area of 7,267 square miles. The surface is mainly rolling with little decided relief. It is partly
timbered with hard woods. The capital is Tishomingo.
Population, white, 124,306; Indian, 5,872; negro, 9,066;
total, 139,260.

Chickasha; post village in Chickasaw Nation on Chicago, Rock
Island and Pacific Railway and on St. Louis and San Francisco Railroad; population, 3,209 .... Chickasha.

Chicken; creek in Creek Nation, a left-hand branch of Little
Deep Fork Creek, a tributary to Deep Fork Canadian River. Nuyaka.

Chickiechockie; post village in Choctaw Nation.

Chigley; post village in Chickasaw Nation.................... Pauls Valley.

Chigley Sandy; creek in Chickasaw Nation, a left-hand branch
of Washita River... Pauls Valley.

Childers; post village in Cherokee Nation.

Childers; creek in Creek Nation, a left-hand branch of Polecat
Creek, a tributary to Arkansas River .... Nuyaka.

Childers; lake in Creek Nation north of Verdigris River....... Claremore.

Chili; station on Missouri, Kansas and Texas Railway.

Chism; post village in Chickasaw Nation.

Chloeta; post village in Cherokee Nation..................... Siloam Springs.

Choate; post village in Choctaw Nation .... Canadian.

Chockie; station on Missouri, Kansas and Texas Railway.

Choctaw Junction; station on St. Louis and San Francisco
Railroad.

Choctaw Nation; reservation in the southeastern part of the
Territory with an area of 10,450 square miles. It is
crossed from east to west by the Ozark Hills, a broad belt
of mountain ridges, which extend into the Territory from
Arkansas. North and south of these mountains the country
is rolling and most of it is well timbered with hard woods.
The capital is Tuskahoma. Population, white, 79,332;
Indian, 10,321; negro, 10,123; total, 99,681.

Choctaw, Oklahoma and Gulf Railroad; now a part of the
Rock Island system, which crosses the Territory from
Mannsville, near Fort Smith, to Oklahoma City.

Choska; post village in Creek Nation......................... Okmulgee.

Choteau; post village in Cherokee Nation on Missouri, Kansas
and Texas Railway .... Pryor.

Choteau; creek in Cherokee Nation, a right-hand branch of
Neosho River .... Pryor.

Chriner; lake in Chickasaw Nation .... Gainesville.

Christie; post village in Cherokee Nation on St. Louis and San
Francisco Railroad.

Chula; post village in Choctaw Nation.

Cimarron; river, a right-hand branch of Arkansas River in
New Mexico, Oklahoma, and Indian Territory. It rises
upon the high plains in two forks in southwestern Colorado
and northwestern New Mexico, and flows with a general
eastward course to its mouth in western Indian Territory.

Citea; post village in Choctaw Nation .... Coalgate.

Civet; post village in Chickasaw Nation.

Claremore; post village in Cherokee Nation on St. Louis and
San Francisco and St. Louis, Iron Mountain and Southern
railroads; population, 855; elevation, 611 feet............. Claremore.

Claremore Mound; summit in Cherokee Nation............. Claremore.

Clarksville; post village in Creek Nation..................... Okmulgee.

Claypool; post village in Chickasaw Nation.

Clayton; station on St. Louis and San Francisco Railroad;
elevation, 598 feet.

Clear; creek in Cherokee Nation, a left-hand branch of Big
Creek, a tributary to Verdigris River .... Vinita.

Clear; creek in Cherokee Nation, a left-hand branch of Neosho
River .... Pryor.

Clear; creek in Chickasaw Nation, a left-hand branch of Mud
Creek, a tributary to Red River .... Addington.

Clear; creek in Chickasaw Nation, a left-hand branch of Wildhorse Creek, a tributary to Washita River .... Rush Springs.

Clear; creek in Choctaw Nation, a left-hand branch of Red {Alikchi.
River. {Clarkesville.

Clear; lake in Choctaw Nation .... Shawneetown.

Clear; lake in Choctaw Nation .... Clarkesville.

Clear Boggy; creek in Choctaw Nation, a right-hand branch of {Atoka.
Boggy Creek, heading in the northern part of Chickasaw {Coalgate.
Nation... {Antlers.

Clear Creek; village in Choctaw Nation...................... Alikchi.

Clearview; post village in Creek Nation.

Cleora; post village in Cherokee Nation.

Cliff; post village in Chickasaw Nation .... Tishomingo.

Clifty; creek in Creek Nation, a left-hand branch of Deep Fork
of Canadian River... Nuyaka.

Cloud; creek in Cherokee Nation, a left-hand branch of Spavinaw Creek .... Siloam Springs.

Cloud; creek in Creek Nation, a right-hand branch of Arkansas
River... Okmulgee.

Clouds; branch in Chickasaw Nation, a left-hand branch of
Red River .... Gainesville.

Cloudy; creek in Choctaw Nation, a right-hand branch of Little
River... Alikchi.

Coal; creek in Cherokee Nation, a right-hand branch of Big
Creek, a tributary to Verdigris River .... Vinita.

Coal; creek in Cherokee Nation, a right-hand branch of Neosho
River... Wyandotte.

Coal; creek in Cherokee and Creek nations, a right-hand branch
of Bird Creek, a tributary to Verdigris River.............. Claremore.

Coal; creek in Chickasaw and Choctaw nations, a right-hand
branch of Clear Boggy Creek.............................. Coalgate.

Coal; creek in Chickasaw Nation, a right-hand branch of Canadian River.. Chickasha.

Coal; creek in Choctaw Nation, a left-hand branch of Gaines {Canadian.
Creek, a tributary to Canadian River. {Coalgate.
{McAlester.

Coal; creek in Choctaw Nation, a left-hand branch of Muddy {Stonewall.
Boggy Creek. {Coalgate.

Coal; creek in Choctaw Nation, a right-hand branch of Cache
Creek, a tributary to Arkansas River........................ Sallisaw.

Coal; creek in Choctaw Nation, a right-hand branch of Muddy
Boggy Creek .... Atoka

Coal; creek in Creek Nation, a left-hand branch of Verdigris
River .... Muscogee.

Coal; creek in Creek Nation, a left-hand branch of Cane Creek,
a tributary to Arkansas River .... Okmulgee.

Coal; creek in Creek Nation, a left-hand branch of Canadian
River .... Wewoka.

Coal; creek in Creek Nation, a left-hand branch of Wolf
Creek, a tributary to North Fork of Canadian River...... Canadian.

Coal; creek in Creek Nation, a right-hand branch of Arkansas {Okmulgee.
River.   {Nuyaka.

Coal Creek; station on Fort Smith and Western and Kansas
City Southern railroads.

Coalgate; post village in Choctaw Nation on Missouri, Kansas
and Texas and Choctaw, Oklahoma and Gulf railroads;
population, 2,614; elevation, 615 feet.

Coata; creek in Creek and Cherokee nations, a right-hand
branch of Arkansas River .... Muscogee.

Coatsworth; post village in Chickasaw Nation.

Coburn; creek in Chickasaw Nation, a right-hand branch of
Washita River .... Ardmore.

Cochran; creek in Chickasaw Nation, a left-hand branch of Red
River.. Gainesville.

Colbert; post village in Chickasaw Nation on Missouri, Kansas
and Texas Railway .... Denison.

Colbert; bridge across Red River in Chickasaw Nation....... Denison.

Colbert; creek in Chickasaw Nation, a left-hand branch of
Washita River.. Rush Springs.

Colbert; crescent-shaped lake in bottom land of Red River in
Choctaw Nation .... Shawneetown.

Coleman; post village in Choctaw Nation.

Collinsville; post village in Cherokee Nation on Atchison,
Topeka and Santa Fe Railway; population 376 .... Claremore.

Comanche; post village in Chickasaw Nation on Chicago,
Rock Island and Pacific Railway; population, 547; elevation, 978 feet.. Addington.

Comeleys; branch in Creek Nation, a left-hand branch of
Little Deep Fork Creek, a tributary to Deep Fork Canadian
River.. Nuyaka.

Compton; small village in Choctaw Nation on St. Louis and San
Francisco Railroad... Tuskahoma.

Concharty; creek in Creek Nation, a right-hand branch of
Arkansas River .... Okmulgee.

Concharty Mountain; summit in Creek Nation.............. Okmulgee.

Conjada Mountain; summit in Creek Nation .... Okmulgee.

Connerville; post village in Chickasaw Nation; population,
189.. Tishomingo.

Conser; post village in Choctaw Nation .... Winding Stair.

Conway; post village in Chickasaw Nation .... Stonewall.

Coodys Bluff; post village in Cherokee Nation .... Nowata.

Cookson; post village in Cherokee Nation on Illinois River... Tahlequah.

Cool; creek in Chickasaw Nation, a right-hand branch of Washita River .... Ardmore.
Coon; creek in Cherokee Nation, a left-hand branch of Caney Creek, a tributary to Verdigris River .... Nowata.
Coon; creek in Chickasaw Nation, a left-hand branch of Sandy Creek, a tributary to Canadian River .... Stonewall.
Coon; creek in Chickasaw Nation, a left-hand branch of Beaver Creek, a tributary to Red River .... Addington.
Coon; creek in Choctaw Nation, a left-hand branch of Caney Creek, a tributary to Muddy Boggy Creek .... Coalgate.
Coon; creek in Choctaw Nation, a right-hand branch of Canadian River.. Coalgate.
Coon; creek in Creek Nation, a right-hand branch of North Fork of Canadian River .... Canadian.
Coon; creek in Seminole Nation, a left-hand branch of Wewoka Creek, a tributary to North Fork of Canadian River ...... Seminole.
Coon; village in Cherokee Nation .... Nowata.
Copan; station on Atchison, Topeka and Santa Fe Railway.
Cope; post village in Chickasaw Nation.
Corcoran; creek in Chickasaw Nation, a left-hand branch of Red River .... Gainesville.
Cornish; post village in Chickasaw Nation; population, 307 .. Addington.
Correta; village in Cherokee Nation on St. Louis and San Francisco Railroad; elevation, 537 feet .... Muscogee.
Cosseetta; creek in Creek Nation, a left-hand branch of Deep Fork of Canadian River.................................... Okmulgee.
Cotton; creek in Cherokee Nation, a left-hand branch of Little Caney Creek, a tributary to Caney River............... Nowata.
Cotton; creek in Chickasaw Nation, a left-hand branch of Beaver Creek, a tributary to Red River.................... Addington.
Cottonwood; creek in Chickasaw Nation, a left-hand branch of Walnut Bayou, a tributary to Red River .... Ardmore.
Cottonwood; post village in Cherokee Nation ...._... Sallisaw.
Cottonwood; village in Choctaw Nation on Missouri, Kansas and Texas Railway....................................... Coalgate.
Coulson; post village in Chickasaw Nation.
Council; isolated hill in Creek Nation........._.............. Okmulgee.
Council House; village in Choctaw Nation .... Tuskahoma.
Court Ground; village in Chickasaw Nation .... Paris.
Courtney; ferry across Red River in Chickasaw Nation ...... Gainesville.
Courtney; post village in Chickasaw Nation........._........ Gainesville.
Courthouse; creek in Cherokee Nation, a right-hand branch ⎰Siloam Springs.
of Narren Creek, a tributary to Illinois River.   ⎱Tahlequah.
Cow; creek in Choctaw Nation, a left-hand branch of Mountain Fork River, a tributary to Little River.................... Winding Stair.
Coweta; creek in Creek Nation, a left-hand branch of Arkansas River .... Okmulgee.
Coweta; post village in Creek Nation on Missouri, Kansas and Texas Railway.. Okmulgee.
Cowlington; post village in Choctaw Nation; population, 272. Sallisaw.
Cowpen; creek in Choctaw Nation, a right-hand branch of Clear Boggy Creek .... Atoka.
Cowper; creek in Choctaw Nation, a right-hand branch of Clear Boggy Creek .... Atoka.

Cowskin; creek in Choctaw Nation, a small left-hand branch of
Sugarloaf Creek, a tributary to Poteau River .... Winding Stair.
Cowskin Prairie; low stretch of land in the northeastern part
of Cherokee Nation... Wyandotte.
Cove; post village in Cherokee Nation........................ Siloam Springs.
Craig; station on Choctow, Oklahoma and Gulf Railroad.
Crassy; lake in Choctaw Nation .... Shawneetown.
Creek; post village in Creek Nation .... Nuyaka.
Creek Nation; reservation in the central part of the Terri-
tory with an area of 5,024 square miles. The surface is
rolling and in some places slightly broken. It is partly tim-
bered with hard woods; the western part is crossed by the
Cross Timbers. The capital is Okmulgee. Population,
white, 25,187; Indian, 7,963; negro, 7,520; total, 40,674.
Criner; creek in Chickasaw Nation, a left-hand branch of $\left\{\begin{array}{l}\text{Rush Springs.}\\\text{Pauls Valley.}\\\text{Chickasha.}\end{array}\right.$
Washita River.
Cripple; creek in Choctaw Nation, a left-hand branch of Black
Fork, a tributary to Little River .... Tuskahoma.
Crittenden; village in Cherokee Nation...................... Muscogee.
Crooked; creek in Chickasaw Nation, a right-hand branch of
Mud Creek, a tributary to Red River...................... Addington.
Crowder; post village in Choctaw Nation on Fort Smith and
Western and Missouri, Kansas and Texas railways.
Crow Hollow; creek in Cherokee Nation, a small intermittent
left-hand branch of Snow Creek, a tributary to Verdigris
River.. Nowata.
Crumb; creek in Choctaw Nation, a left-hand branch of Kiami- $\left\{\begin{array}{l}\text{McAlester.}\\\text{Tuskahoma.}\end{array}\right.$
chi River.
Cucumber; creek in Choctaw Nation, a left-hand branch of
Eagle Fork, a tributary to Mountain Fork River .... Winding Stair.
Cumberland; post village in Chickasaw Nation; population, 343. Tishomingo.
Cummins; village in Creek Nation........................... Canadian.
Curl; creek in Cherokee Nation, a left-hand branch of Caney
River, a tributary to Verdigris River .... Nowata.
Cut Off; lake in Choctaw Nation............................ Clarkesville.
Cut Off; lake in Choctaw Nation............................ Shawneetown.
Damon; post village in Choctaw Nation...................... Tuskahoma.
Darrow; station on St. Louis and San Francisco Railroad.
Davenport; station on St. Louis and San Francisco Railroad;
elevation, 473 feet.
David; village in Cherokee Nation........................... Vinita.
Davis; post village in Chickasaw Nation on Gulf, Colorado $\left\{\begin{array}{l}\text{Ardmore.}\\\text{Pauls Valley.}\end{array}\right.$
and Santa Fe Railway.
Davis; ferry across Clear Boggy Creek, in Choctaw Nation .... Atoka.
Dawes; post village in Cherokee Nation.
Dawson; post village in Cherokee Nation on St. Louis and San
Francisco Railroad .... Claremore.
Days; creek in Chickasaw Nation, a right-hand branch of
Sandy Creek, a tributary to Canadian River.............. Stonewall.
Decherds; bend in Red River in Chickasaw Nation.......... Gainesville.
Deep; creek in Cherokee Nation, a left-hand branch of Illinois
River, a tributary to Arkansas River..................... Muscogee.

Deep; creek in Creek Nation, a left-hand branch of Little River, a tributary to Canadian River...................... Wewoka.

Deep Fork of Canadian; river, a left-hand branch of North Fork of Canadian River, heading in Oklahoma Territory and flowing east and then south through Creek Nation. {Canadian. Nuyaka. Okmulgee.

Deer; creek in Chickasaw Nation, a left-hand branch of Mud Creek, a tributary to Red River, heading in South Fork... Addington.

Deer; creek in Seminole Nation, a right-hand branch of North Fork of Canadian River.................................... Seminole.

Delaware; creek in Cherokee Nation, a right-hand branch of Bird Creek, a tributary to Verdigris River .... Claremore.

Delaware; creek in Choctaw Nation, a right-hand branch of Clear Boggy Creek. {Tishomingo. Atoka.

Delaware; post village in Cherokee Nation on St. Louis, Iron Mountain and Southern Railway .... Nowata.

Demijohn; creek in Chickasaw Nation, a right-hand branch of Walnut Bayou, a tributary to Red River................ Ardmore.

Depew; post village in Creek Nation.

Dewey; post village in Cherokee Nation on Atchison, Topeka and Santa Fe Railway.

Dexter; post village in Choctaw Nation on St. Louis and San Francisco Railroad ---------------------------------- Tuskahoma.

Diamond Spring; branch in Chickasaw Nation, a right-hand branch of Blue River .... Tishomingo.

Dibble; creek in Chickasaw Nation, a right-hand branch of Walnut Creek, a tributary to Canadian River.............. Chickasha.

Dibble; post village in Chickasaw Nation..................... Chickasha.

Dirteater; ford across Neosho River in Cherokee Nation..... Pryor.

Dirty; creek, a right-hand branch of Arkansas River .... {Sansbois. Muscogee.

Diver; creek in Cherokee Nation, a right-hand branch of Pryor Creek, a tributary to Neosho River .... Pryor.

Dixie; post village in Chickasaw Nation...................... Addington.

Doaksville; creek in Choctaw Nation, a left-hand branch of Red River. {Alikchi. Clarkesville.

Doaksville; village in Choctaw Nation....................... Alikchi.

Dodge; post village in Cherokee Nation on St. Louis and San Francisco Railroad.

Dog; creek in Cherokee Nation, a right-hand branch of Panther Creek, a tributary to Verdigris River. {Pryor. Claremore.

Dog; creek in Creek Nation, a right-hand branch of Polecat Creek, a tributary to Arkansas River .... Nuyaka.

Dolan; station on Missouri, Kansas and Texas Railway; elevation, 517 feet.

Dolberg; post village in Chickasaw Nation.................... Stonewall.

Double; creek in Cherokee Nation, a right-hand branch of Verdigris River, heading in North and South forks .... Nowata.

Double; creek in Cherokee Nation, a right-hand branch of Caney River, heading in North and South forks .... Nowata.

Double Spring; creek in Cherokee Nation, a left-hand branch of Fourteenmile Creek, a tributary to Neosho River ...... Muscogee.

Double Spring; creek in Cherokee Nation, a right-hand branch of Spring Creek, a tributary to Neosho River. {Pryor. Siloam Springs.

Dougherty; post village in Chickasaw Nation on Gulf, Colorado and Santa Fe Railway; elevation, 775 feet........... Ardmore.

Dow; post village in Choctaw Nation on Choctaw, Oklahoma
and Gulf Railroad.

Doyle; post village in Chickasaw Nation.................... Rush Springs.

Drake; post village in Chickasaw Nation on St. Louis and San
Francisco Railroad.

Dripping Springs; branch in Cherokee Nation, a right-hand
branch of Illinois River, a tributary to Arkansas River.... Siloam Springs.

Dripping Springs; village in Cherokee Nation .... Siloam Springs.

Drowning; creek in Cherokee Nation, a small left-hand branch ⎰Siloam Springs.
of Neosho River.   ⎱Wyandotte.

Dry; creek in Cherokee Nation, a left-hand branch of Spavinaw Creek, a tributary to Neosho River.......... .... Siloam Springs.

Dry; creek in Chickasaw Nation, a right-hand branch of Washita River.. Rush Springs.

Dry; creek in Chickasaw Nation, a left-hand branch of Walnut
Bayou, a tributary to Red River........................... Gainesville.

Dry; creek in Choctaw Nation, a left-hand branch of Mountain
Fork, a tributary to Little River......................... Lukfata.

Duchess; creek in Cherokee Nation, a left-hand branch of
Canadian River .... Sansbois.

Duck; creek in Cherokee Nation, a right-hand branch of Neosho River... Wyandotte.

Duck; creek in Creek Nation, a left-hand branch of Snake ⎱Okmulgee.
Creek, a tributary to Arkansas River, heading in North, ⎰Nuyaka.
South, and Middle Duck Creek.

Dumpling; creek in Choctaw Nation, a right-hand tributary
to Kiamichi River....................................... Antlers.

Duncan; post village in Chickasaw Nation on Chicago, Rock
Island and Pacific Railway; population, 1,164; elevation,
1,126 feet .... Rush Springs.

Dunford; creek in Choctaw Nation, a left-hand branch of
Boggy Creek... Coalgate.

Durant; post village in Choctaw Nation on Missouri, Kansas
and Texas and St. Louis and San Francisco railroads; population, 2,969; elevation, 643 feet...................... Bonham.

Durwood; post village in Chickasaw Nation on Choctaw, Oklahoma and Gulf Railroad .... Tishomingo.

Dwight; post village in Choctaw Nation.

Eagle; creek in Creek Nation, a right-hand branch of Duck ⎱Okmulgee.
Creek, a tributary to Arkansas River.   ⎰Nuyaka.

Eagle; fork in Choctaw Nation, a right-hand branch of Moun- ⎱Lukfata.
tain Fork River, a tributary to Little River.   ⎰Winding Stair.

Eagle; post village in Cherokee Nation...................... Vinita.

Eagle Bend; lake in Choctaw Nation north of Red River..... Shawneetown.

Eaglepoint; post village in Choctaw Nation.

Eagletown; post village in Choctaw Nation near Mountain
Fork River... Lukfata.

Earbob; ferry across the Neosho River in Cherokee Nation... Pryor.

Earl; post village in Chickasaw Nation; population, 225...... Tishomingo.

East; creek in Cherokee Nation, a right-hand branch of Caney
River, a tributary to Verdigris River..................... Claremore.

East; fork in Cherokee Nation, a left-hand branch of Big Creek. Vinita.

East; fork in Choctaw Nation, a left-hand branch of Glover
  Creek, a tributary to Little River......................... Lukfata.
East; fork in Choctaw Nation, a left-hand branch of Muddy
  Boggy Creek .... Coalgate.
East Beaver or Cow; creek in Chickasaw Nation, a left-hand
  branch of Beaver Creek, a tributary to Red River .... Addington.
East Blue; river in Chickasaw Nation, a left-hand branch of
  Blue River.. Tishomingo.
East Cabin; creek in Cherokee Nation, a right-hand branch
  of Little Cabin Creek, a tributary to Neosho River........ Vinita.
East Cow; creek in Chickasaw Nation, a left-hand branch of
  Beaver Creek, a tributary to Red River .... Addington.
East Little Polecat; creek in Creek Nation, a left-hand branch
  of Polecat Creek, a tributary to Arkansas River. .... Nuyaka.
East Peavine; creek in Chickasaw Nation, a left-hand branch
  of Peavine Creek, a tributary to Washita River........... Pauls Valley.
Eastman; post village in Chickasaw Nation .... Gainesville.
Eaton; post village in Cherokee Nation.
Echo; post village in Cherokee Nation........................ Wyandotte.
Econtuchka; village in Seminole Nation..................... Seminole.
Edna; post village in Creek Nation.
Edwards; post village in Choctaw Nation on Choctaw, Okla-
  homa and Gulf Railroad.
Ego; post village in Choctaw Nation.
Eightmile; creek in Chickasaw Nation, a right-hand branch of {Ardmore.
  Wildhorse Creek, a tributary to Washita River.   {Pauls Valley.
Elam; post village in Creek Nation.
Elba; station on St. Louis, Iron Mountain and Southern
  Railway.
Eli; village in Cherokee Nation............................ Claremore.
Elk; post village in Chickasaw Nation........................ Ardmore.
Elk; creek in Cherokee Nation, a left-hand branch of Illinois
  River... Tahlequah.
                                                        {Muscogee.
Elk; creek in Creek Nation, a right-hand branch of Dirty {Sansbois.
  Creek, a tributary to Arkansas River.   {Canadian.
                                                        {Okmulgee.
Elkhorn Prairie; low stretch of land south of Spavinaw Creek
  in Cherokee Nation...................................... Siloam Springs.
Elliott; post village in Cherokee Nation on St. Louis, Iron
  Mountain and Southern Railway .... Nowata.
Elm; creek in Cherokee Nation, a left-hand branch of Bird
  Creek, a tributary to Verdigris River .... Claremore.
Elm; creek in Cherokee Nation, an intermittent right-hand
  branch of Holly Creek, a tributary to Neosho River ...... Wyandotte.
Elm; creek in Cherokee Nation, a right-hand branch of Russell
  Creek, a tributary to Neosho River...................... Vinita.
Elm; creek in Choctaw Nation, a small right-hand branch of
  Emachaya Creek, a tributary to Canadian River.......... Sansbois.
Elm; creek in Choctaw Nation, a right-hand branch of Gaines {Canadian.
  Creek, a tributary to Canadian River.   {Sansbois.
Elm; creek in Choctaw Nation, a right-hand branch of Brushy
  Creek, a tributary to Gaines Creek .... McAlester.

Elzey; village in Choctaw Nation on St. Louis and San Francisco Railroad .... Tuskahoma.
Emachaya; creek in Choctaw Nation, a right-hand branch of Canadian River .... Sansbois.
Emahaka; post village in Seminole Nation.
Emet; post village in Chickasaw Nation; population, 342 ...... Tishomingo.
Enterprise; post village in Choctaw Nation .... Sansbois.
Erin Springs; post village in Chickasaw Nation.............. Rush Springs.
Estella; post village in Cherokee Nation.
Etna; village in Choctaw Nation.......................... McAlester.
Eucha; post village in Cherokee Nation.
Euchre; creek in Creek Nation, a right-hand branch of Polecat Creek, a tributary to Arkansas River .... Nuyaka.
Eufaula; town in Creek Nation, on Missouri, Kansas and Texas Railway; population, 757 .... Canadian.
Eureka; post village in Cherokee Nation.
Evansville; creek in Cherokee Nation, a left-hand branch of Barren Fork, a tributary to Illinois River................. Tahlequah.
Everidge; lake in Choctaw Nation........................... Clarkesville.
Fagan; creek in Cherokee Nation, a fork of Flint Creek, a tributary to Illinois River................................. Siloam Springs.
Fairland; post village in Cherokee Nation on St. Louis and San Francisco Railroad; population, 499................... Wyandotte.
Fall; branch in Cherokee Nation, an intermittent left-hand branch of Illinois River, a tributary to Arkansas River ... Siloam Springs.
Falls; branch in Cherokee Nation, an intermittent right-hand branch of Illinois River, a tributary to Arkansas River ... Siloam Springs.
Fame; post village in Creek Nation .... Canadian.
Fanshawe; post village in Choctaw Nation on Choctaw, Oklahoma and Gulf Railroad; population, 542................. Winding Stair.
Farmers; post village in Choctaw Nation .... Sallisaw.
Farris; post village in Choctaw Nation.
Fawn; post village in Cherokee Nation.
Featherstown; post village in Choctaw Nation .... Sansbois.
Fentress; post village in Creek Nation on North Fork of Canadian River .... Wewoka.
Fillmore; post village in Chickasaw Nation.
Finley; post village in Choctaw Nation.
Fish; creek in Cherokee Nation, a left-hand branch of Caney River, a tributary to Verdigris River .... Nowata.
Fish; creek in Chickasaw Nation, a left-hand branch of Black Bear Creek, a tributary to Washita River .... Rush Springs.
Fish; creek in Chickasaw Nation, a left-hand branch of Washita River... Pauls Valley.
Fish; creek in Choctaw Nation, a small left-hand branch of Sansbois Creek, a tributary to Arkansas River............. Sansbois.
Fish; creek in Creek Nation, a right-hand branch of North Fork of Canadian River................................... Wewoka.
Fish; creek in Creek Nation, a right-hand branch of Wewoka Creek, a tributary to North Fork of Canadian River....... Wewoka.
Fishing; creek in Seminole Nation, a right-hand branch of North Fork of Canadian River............................. Seminole.
Fishertown; village in Creek Nation.......................... Canadian.
Fitzhugh; post village in Chickasaw Nation................. Stonewall.

Flat; creek in Chickasaw Nation, a left-hand branch of Beaver { Addington.
Creek, a tributary to Red River. { Montague.

Flat Rock; creek in Cherokee Nation, a right-hand branch of
Bird Creek, a tributary to Verdigris River................ Claremore.

Flat Rock; creek in Cherokee and Creek nations, a right-hand
branch of Neosho River................................... Pryor.

Flat Rock; creek in Creek Nation, a left-hand branch of
Deep Fork of Canadian River, heading in West and East
branches.. Nuyaka.

Flat Rock; creek in Creek Nation, a left-hand branch of Mill
Creek, a tributary to Canadian River .... Canadian.

Flat Rock; creek in Creek Nation, a left-hand branch of North
Fork of Canadian River................................... Wewoka.

Fleetwood; post village in Chickasaw Nation................. Montague.

Flint; creek in Cherokee Nation, a right-hand branch of Illinois River, a tributary to Arkansas River .... Siloam Springs.

Flint; post village in Cherokee Nation...................... Tahlequah.

Flower; creek in Cherokee Nation, a left-hand branch of
Neosho River, a tributary to Arkansas River .... Muscogee.

Fly; creek in Cherokee Nation, a right-hand branch of Neosho
River.. Wyandotte.

Folsom; post village in Choctaw Nation on St. Louis and San
Francisco Railroad; elevation, 494 feet .... Atoka.

Fool; creek in Cherokee Nation, a left-hand branch of Verdigris River... Nowata.

Foreman; post village in Cherokee Nation.

Forney; post village in Choctaw Nation.

Fort Gibson; post village in Cherokee Nation on St. Louis and
San Francisco Railroad; population, 617; elevation, 536 feet. Muscogee.

Fort Towson; post village in Choctaw Nation on St. Louis and
San Francisco Railroad.

Foster; post village in Chickasaw Nation.................... Pauls Valley.

Fourche Maline; right-hand branch of Poteau River in Choc- { Tuskahoma.
taw Nation. { Winding Stair.

Fourmile; branch in Cherokee Nation, a right-hand branch of
Bayou Manard, a tributary to Neosho River.............. Muscogee.

Fourmile; creek in Cherokee Nation, a left-hand branch of
Caney River, a tributary to Verdigris River .... Nowata.

Fourmile; creek in Cherokee Nation, a right-hand branch of
Coon Creek, a tributary to Caney River .... Nowata.

Fourmile; creek in Cherokee Nation, a right-hand branch of { Nowata.
Verdigris River, a tributary to Arkansas River. { Claremore.

Fourteenmile; creek in Cherokee Nation, a left-hand branch { Pryor.
of Neosho River. { Muscogee.
{ Silom Springs.

Fox; post village in Chickasaw Nation .... Ardmore.

Foyil; post village in Cherokee Nation on Oklahoma Division
of St. Louis and San Francisco Railroad .... Claremore.

Francis; post village in Chickasaw Nation on St. Louis and San
Francisco Railroad.

Frank Henry; creek in Creek Nation, a right-hand branch of
Little Deep Fork of Canadian River, a tributary to Deep
Fork of Canadian River................................... Nuyaka.

Franks; post village in Chickasaw Nation................... Stonewall.

Frazier; branch in Cherokee Nation, a right-hand branch of
  Cabin Creek, a tributary to Neosho River .... Vinita.
Frazier; left-hand branch of Kiamichi River in Choctaw Nation. Winding Stair.
Frazier; creek in Choctaw Nation, a right-hand branch of
  Spencer Creek, a tributary to Kiamichi River .... Alikchi.
Freeo; village in Chickasaw Nation.......................... Addington.
French's; ferry (two, upper and lower) across the Neosho
  River in Cherokee Nation................................. Muscogee.
Frink; station on Missouri, Kansas and Texas Railway.
Fry; post village in Creek Nation.

Gaines; creek in Choctaw Nation, a large right-hand branch of $\begin{cases} \text{Canadian.} \\ \text{Tuskahoma.} \\ \text{McAlester.} \end{cases}$ Canadian River.

Gans; post village in Cherokee Nation on Kansas City South-
  ern Railway; population, 136 .... Sallisaw.
Gap; creek in Choctaw Nation, a left-hand branch of Poteau $\begin{cases} \text{Fort Smith.} \\ \text{Sallisaw.} \end{cases}$
  River, heading in Arkansas.
Gap; station on Missouri, Kansas and Texas Railway.
Gar; creek in Creek Nation, a right-hand branch of Verdigris
  River .... Okmulgee.
Gar; fork in Seminole Nation, a left-hand branch of Fishing
  Creek, a tributary to North Fork of Canadian River ...... Seminole.
Garfield; village in Cherokee Nation .... Muscogee.
Garland; post village in Choctaw Nation.................... Sansbois.
Garland; creek in Choctaw Nation, a left-hand branch of Red
  River .... Clarkesville.
Garner; post village in Choctaw Nation on Fort Smith and
  Western Railroad.
Garnet; station on St. Louis and San Francisco Railroad.
Garrison; creek in Cherokee Nation, a left-hand branch of $\begin{cases} \text{Fort Smith.} \\ \text{Sallisaw.} \end{cases}$
  Lee's Creek, a tributary to Arkansas River.
Garrison; post village in Cherokee Nation.
Garvin; creek in Choctaw Nation, a left-hand branch of Red
  River .... Shawneetown.
Garvin; post village in Choctaw Nation on St. Louis and San
  Francisco Railroad....................................... Shawneetown.
Gates; creek in Choctaw Nation, a left-hand branch of Kiami-
  chi River .... Alikchi.
Gatesville; post village in Creek Nation.
Gaylor; ferry across Neosho River in Cherokee Nation .... Pryor.
Gibson; creek in Choctaw Nation, a left-hand branch of Gaines
  Creek, a tributary to Canadian River .... Canadian.
Gibson Station; post village in Creek Nation on Missouri,
  Kansas and Texas Railway; elevation, 532 feet........... Muscogee.
Gideon; post village in Cherokee Nation .... Pryor.
Gilbert; station on St. Louis and San Francisco Railroad.
Gilmore; post village in Choctaw Nation.................... Sallisaw.
Gilsonite; post village in Chickasaw Nation .... Tishomingo.
Glasby; branch in Cherokee Nation, a fork of Flint Creek, a
  tributary to Illinois River .... Siloam Springs.
Glasses; creek in Chickasaw Nation, a right-hand branch of
  Washita River .... Tishomingo.
Glenn; post village in Chickasaw Nation .... Ardmore.

Globe; post village in Choctaw Nation .... Coalgate.

Glover; creek in Choctaw Nation, a left-hand branch of Little
River, heading in East and West Forks.................... Lukfata.

Glover; post village in Choctaw Nation.

Gobbler; creek in Creek Nation, a left-hand branch of Canadian River.. Wewoka.

Going Snake; village in Cherokee Nation .... Tahlequah.

Golconda; post village in Choctaw Nation .... Sansbois.

Goodland; town in Choctaw Nation on St. Louis and Paris
Division of St. Louis and San Francisco Railroad; elevation,
504 feet... Antlers.

Goodspring; post village in Choctaw Nation.

Goodwater; creek in Choctaw Nation, a right-hand branch of
Little River .... Shawneetown.

Goodwater; creek in Choctaw Nation, a left-hand branch of
Red River .... Clarkesville.

Goodwater; post village in Choctaw Nation .... Shawneetown.

Goose; creek in Choctaw and Chickasaw nations, a right-hand {Stonewall.
branch of Clear Boggy Creek.   {Coalgate.

Gordon; village in Choctaw Nation .... Tuskahoma.

Gowen; post village in Choctaw Nation ....{McAlester.
                                                              {Tuskahoma.

Grady; post village in Chickasaw Nation .... Addington.

Graham; post village in Chickasaw Nation .... Ardmore.

Grant; post village in Choctaw Nation on St. Louis and San
Francisco Railroad .... Paris.

Grantham; village in Chickasaw Nation .... Tishomingo.

Grassy; lake in Choctaw Nation............................. Clarkesville.

Grassy; lake in Choctaw Nation............................. Shawneetown.

Grave; creek in Creek Nation, a left-hand branch of Deep Fork
of Canadian River.. Okmulgee.

Grave; creek in Creek Nation, a right-hand branch of Grief
Creek, a tributary to North Fork of Canadian River ...... Wewoka.

Grayson; creek in Chickasaw Nation, a right-hand branch of
Canadian River .... Stonewall.

Grayson; post village in Creek Nation.

Greasy; creek in Cherokee Nation, a left-hand branch of Sallisaw Creek, a tributary to Arkansas River .... Tahlequah.

Greasy; creek in Creek Nation, a right-hand branch of Wewoka
Creek, a tributary to North Fork of Canadian River ...... Wewoka.

Greenbrier; post village in Cherokee Nation.

Greenleaf; creek in Cherokee Nation, a left-hand branch of
Arkansas River .... Muscogee.

Greenville; post village in Chickasaw Nation.

Greenwood; branch in Choctaw Nation, a left-hand branch of
Delaware Creek, tributary to Clear Boggy Creek.......... Atoka.

Greenwood; village in Chickasaw Nation .... Tishomingo.

Grief; creek in Creek Nation, a right-hand branch of Wewoka
Creek, a tributary to North Fork of Canadian River ...... Wewoka.

Gritts; post village in Cherokee Nation...................... Sansbois.

Grove; post village in Cherokee Nation on St. Louis and San
Francisco Railroad; population, 314....................... Wyandotte.

Guertie; post village in Choctaw Nation .... Coalgate.

Gulf, Colorado and Santa Fe Railway; part of the Santa Fe System, crossing Chickasaw Nation from Purcell through Ardmore to Texas.

Gum Spring; village in Chickasaw Nation .... Tishomingo.

Guy Sandy; creek in Chickasaw Nation, a left-hand branch of Big Sandy Creek, a tributary to Washita River........... Stonewall.

Gwenndale; post village in Cherokee Nation on St. Louis and San Francisco Railroad .... Vinita.

Hadley; post village in Cherokee Nation.

Haileyville; post village in Choctaw Nation on Choctaw, Oklahoma and Gulf Railroad.

Hails; station on St. Louis and San Francisco Railroad.

Haley; station on St. Louis and San Francisco Railroad.

Halleman; post village in Choctaw Nation.

Hamden; post village in Choctaw Nation on St. Louis and San Francisco Railroad......................... .... Antlers.

Hamilton; station on St. Louis and San Francisco Railroad.

Handy; post village in Creek Nation.

Hanson; post village in Cherokee Nation on St. Louis, Iron Mountain and Southern Railway; population, 182 .... Sallisaw.

Hardscrabble; a peak in the Williams Mountains in Choctaw Nation.. Lukfata.

Harlins; ferry across Neosho River in Cherokee Nation...... Wyandotte.

Harrington; station on St. Louis and San Francisco Railroad.

Harris; ferry across Red River in Choctaw Nation .... Shawneetown.

Harris; ferry across Verdigris River in Creek Nation......... Muscogee.

Harris; post village in Choctaw Nation...................... Shawneetown.

Harris Bayou; left-hand branch of Red River in Choctaw Nation.. Shawneetown.

Harrisburg; post village in Chickasaw Nation.

Harris Eagle; station on Kansas City Southern Railway.

Hart; post village in Chickasaw Nation...................... Stonewall.

Hartshorne; town in Choctaw Nation on Choctaw, Oklahoma and Gulf Railroad; population, 2,352; elevation, 704 feet... McAlester.

Hasson; post village in Creek Nation.

Hastings; station on St. Louis and San Francisco Railroad.

Hauto; station on St. Louis, Iron Mountain and Southern Railway.

Hawani; creek in Chickasaw Nation, a left-hand branch of Red River .... Denison.

Haws; creek in Choctaw Nation, heading in Arkansas, a left-hand branch of Black Fork, a tributary to Poteau River. {Winding Stair. Poteau.

Hayden; post village in Cherokee Nation .... Vinita.

Hay Ranch; station on Choctaw, Oklahoma and Gulf Railroad.

Hazelnut Hollow; valley of Hazelnut Creek, a left-hand branch of Flint Creek, a tributary to Illinois River, in Cherokee Nation .... Siloam Springs.

Healdton; post village in Chickasaw Nation .... Ardmore.

Heavener; post village in Choctaw Nation on Kansas City Southern Railway; population, 234 .... Winding Stair.

Helen; station on St. Louis and San Francisco Railroad.

Heliswa; village in Seminole Nation......................... Seminole.

Hennepin; post village in Chickasaw Nation .... Pauls Valley.

Henryetta; post village in Creek Nation on St. Louis and San Francisco Railroad.

Henry House; creek in Chickasaw Nation, a left-hand branch of Caddo Creek, a tributary to Washita River .... Ardmore.

Henubby; left-hand branch of Red River in Chickasaw Nation. Paris.

Herbert; post village in Choctaw Nation on Choctaw, Oklahoma and Gulf Railroad.

Hereford; post village in Cherokee Nation.

Hewitt; post village in Chickasaw Nation................... Ardmore.

Hickman; village in Choctaw Nation......................... Sallisaw.

Hickory; creek in Cherokee Nation, a right-hand branch of Neosho River .... Wyandotte.

Hickory; creek in Cherokee Nation, a right-hand branch of Verdigris River, a tributary to Arkansas River .... Nowata.

Hickory; creek in Chickasaw Nation, a left-hand branch of Red River. $\left\{\begin{array}{l}\text{Denison.}\\\text{Gainesville.}\\\text{Ardmore.}\end{array}\right.$

Hickory; creek in Chickasaw Nation, a left-hand branch of Caddo Creek, a tributary to Washita River................ Ardmore.

Hickory; post village in Chickasaw Nation on St. Louis and San Francisco Railroad; population, 262 .... Stonewall.

Higgins; post village in Choctaw Nation.

Hillside; post village in Cherokee Nation .... Claremore.

Hird; village in Chickasaw Nation.......................... Stonewall.

Hitchita; post village in Creek Nation.

Hochetown; post village in Choctaw Nation................. Lukfata.

Hog; creek in Cherokee Nation, a small right-hand branch of $\left\{\begin{array}{l}\text{Sallisaw.}\\\text{Tahlequah.}\end{array}\right.$ Little Sallisaw Creek, a tributary to Arkansas River.

Hogshooter; creek in Cherokee Nation, a left-hand branch of Caney Creek, a tributary to Verdigris River.............. Nowata.

Holden; station on Choctaw, Oklahoma and Gulf Railroad.

Holdenville; post village in Creek Nation on Choctaw, Oklahoma and Gulf and St. Louis and San Francisco railroads; population, 749... Wewoka.

Holder; post village in Chickasaw Nation .... Denison.

Holly; creek in Cherokee Nation, a left-hand branch of Neosho River .... Wyandotte.

Holly; creek in Choctaw Nation, a left-hand branch of Little $\left\{\begin{array}{l}\text{Shawneetown.}\\\text{Lukfata.}\end{array}\right.$ River.

Holson; station on Choctaw, Oklahoma and Gulf Railroad.

Holston; creek in Choctaw Nation, a left-hand branch of Fourche Maline, a tributary to Poteau River .... Winding Stair.

Homer; post village in Chickasaw Nation .... Ardmore.

Hominy; creek in Cherokee Nation, a right-hand branch of Bird Creek, a tributary to Verdigris River .... Claremore.

Honey; creek in Chickasaw Nation, a right-hand branch of Washita River .... Ardmore.

Honey; creek in Chickasaw Nation, a left-hand branch of Salt Creek, a tributary through Wildhorse Creek to Washita River... Pauls Valley.

Honey; creek in Creek Nation, a right-hand branch of Deep Fork of Canadian River..................................... Nuyaka.

Hooper; creek in Creek Nation, a left-hand branch of Deep Fork of Canadian River .... Nuyaka.

Hope; post village in Chickasaw Nation....................... Rush Springs.

Horse; creek in Cherokee Nation, a right-hand branch of Neosho River... Wyandotte.

Horse; creek in Chickasaw Nation, a left-hand branch of Red River... Paris.

Horsepen; creek in Cherokee Nation, a right-hand branch of Caney River, a tributary to Verdigris River............... Claremore.

Horsepen; creek in Choctaw Nation, a left-hand branch of Little River... Lukfata.

Horse Shoe; bend in Red River in Chickasaw Nation........ Gainesville.

Horseshoe; lake in Cherokee Nation, cut-off from Neosho River... Muscogee.

Horseshoe; lake in Cherokee Nation near Neosho River ..... Wyandotte.

Horse Shoe; lake in Choctaw Nation .... Shawneetown.

Horseshoe; lake in Creek Nation, cut-off from North Fork of Canadian River .... Canadian.

House; creek in Chickasaw Nation, a left-hand branch of Red ⎰Tishomingo.
River.   ⎱Denison.

House; creek in Choctaw Nation, a left-hand branch of Long-⎰Sansbois.
town Creek, a tributary to Canadian River.   ⎱Canadian.

Houston; village in Choctaw Nation on Kansas City Southern Railway .... Winding Stair.

Howe; post village in Choctaw Nation on Kansas City Southern Railway; population, 626............................. Winding Stair.

Hoxbar; post village in Chickasaw Nation.................... Ardmore.

Hoyt; post village in Choctaw Nation........................ Sansbois.

Hudson; creek, a right-hand branch of Grand River, Cherokee Nation... Wyandotte.

Hudson; creek in Choctaw Nation, a right-hand branch of Mountain Fork River, a tributary to Little River......... Lukfata.

Hudson; post village in Cherokee Nation .... Vinita.

Hughes; post village in Choctaw Nation on Choctaw, Oklahoma and Gulf Railroad.

Hugo; post village in Choctaw Nation on St. Louis and San Francisco Railroad.

Hulbert; post village in Cherokee Nation.

Hunton; post village in Chickasaw Nation .... Atoka.

Hurd; creek in Choctaw Nation, a right-hand branch of Kiamichi River .... Tuskahoma.

Huttonville; post village in Creek Nation.

Illinois; station on St. Louis, Iron Mountain and Southern Railway; elevation, 495 feet.

Illinois; river, a left-hand branch of Neosho River. It heads⎰Tahlequah.
in the Ozark Hills in northwestern Arkansas and flows⎨Muscogee.
southwest to its mouth in Cherokee Nation.   ⎩Siloam Springs.

Indiangrave Hollow; valley of Indiangrave Creek, a right-hand branch of Illinois River, in Cherokee Nation........ Siloam Springs.

Indianola; post village in Choctaw Nation on Fort Smith and Western Railroad .... Canadian.

Inola; post village in Creek Nation on St. Louis, Iron Mountain and Southern Railway; elevation, 600 feet................ Claremore.

Iona; post village in Chickasaw Nation....................... Pauls Valley.

Irene; post village in Creek Nation.

Ireton; post village in Chickasaw Nation .... Rush Springs.

Iron Bridge; post village in Choctaw Nation .... Sallisaw.

Iroquois; station on Gulf, Colorado and Santa Fe Railway.

Island; ferry across Verdigris River in Cherokee Nation...... Claremore.

Island; ford across Neosho River in Cherokee Nation .... Pryor.

Island Bayou; left-hand branch of Red River in Choctaw and
    Chickasaw nations .... Bonham.

Isom Springs; post village in Chickasaw Nation.

Jackford; creek in Chickasaw Nation, a right-hand branch of
    Clear Boggy Creek, heading in North and South Fork.... Stonewall.

Jackford; creek in Choctaw Nation, a left-hand branch of
    Kiamichi River .... Tuskahoma.

Jackford; mountains in Choctaw Nation, a ridge of the Ozark (Tuskahoma.
    Hills trending northeast and southwest; altitude, 1,550 feet. (McAlester.

Jackson; branch in Choctaw Nation, a right-hand branch of
    Rock Creek, a tributary to Kiamichi River................ Tuskahoma.

Jackson; creek in Choctaw Nation, a small right-hand branch
    of Canadian River.. Sansbois.

Jackson; post village in Chickasaw Nation .... Paris.

James; creek in Choctaw Nation, a left-hand branch of Little
    River.. Winding Stair.

James; fork in Choctaw Nation, a left-hand branch of Poteau (Sallisaw.
    River, heading in Arkansas and flowing west into Indian (Fort Smith.
    Territory.

Jane Dennis; creek in Cherokee Nation, a small left-hand
    branch of Neosho River................................... Pryor.

Janis; post village in Choctaw Nation.................... Shawneetown.

Jefferson; creek in Choctaw Nation, a left-hand branch of (Sallisaw.
    Brazil Creek, a tributary to Poteau River.   (Sansbois.

Jeffs; post village in Chickasaw Nation...................... Coalgate.

Jenkins; creek in Cherokee Nation, a small left-hand branch
    of Lee Creek, a tributary to Arkansas River.............. Tahlequah.

Jerrys; branch in Chickasaw Nation, a small right-hand branch
    of Shiggin Creek, a tributary to Red River............... Gainesville.

Jesse; post village in Chickasaw Nation..................... Stonewall.

Jimtown; village in Chickasaw Nation....................... Gainesville.

Johnson; post village in Chickasaw Nation, population, 204.. Pauls Valley.

Johnson Prairie; low stretch of land in Cherokee Nation,
    northwest of Illinois River............................. Siloam Springs.

Johnsonville; station on Missouri, Kansas and Texas Railway

Johnstown; village in Choctaw Nation on Missouri, Kansas
    and Texas Railway.. McAlester.

Jones; creek in Choctaw Nation, a right-hand branch of Gaines
    Creek, a tributary to Canadian River .... Canadian.

Juanita; post village in Choctaw Nation.

Jumper; creek in Seminole Nation, a right-hand branch of
    Canadian River .... Stonewall.

Kali Tukelo; village in Choctaw Nation .... Shawneetown.

Kannalla; creek in Choctaw Nation, a right-hand branch of
    Blue River... Bonham.

Kansas; creek in Chickasaw Nation, a left-hand branch of
    Washita River .... Tishomingo.

Kansas; post village in Cherokee Nation.................... Siloam Springs.

Kansas City Southern Railway, extending from Kansas City to Port Arthur, Tex., traversing the eastern edge of the Territory.

Katie; post village in Chickasaw Nation .... Pauls Valley.

Kavanaugh; mountains with summits in Choctaw Nation ... Sallisaw.

Keeler; creek in Cherokee Nation, a right-hand branch of Caney River, a tributary to Verdigris River .... Nowata.

Keil Sandy; creek in Chickasaw Nation, a right-hand branch of Cherokee Sandy Creek, a tributary to Washita River... Pauls Valley.

Keller; post village in Chickasaw Nation..................... Ardmore.

Kellyville; post village in Creek Nation on St. Louis and San Francisco Railroad .... Nuyaka.

Kelso; post village in Cherokee Nation on Missouri, Kansas and Texas Railway....................................... Vinita.

Keltner; village in Chickasaw Nation........................ Gainesville.

Kemp; post village in Chickasaw Nation; population, 221..... Bonham.

Kennady; post village in Choctaw Nation on Mountain Creek, a tributary to Poteau River............................... Sallisaw.

Kentucky; creek in Cherokee Nation, a right-hand branch of Salt Creek, a tributary to Verdigris River................. Nowata.

Kerk; post village in Cherokee Nation.

Kiamichi; an east-west ridge of the Ozark Hills in Choctaw Nation, south of Kiamichi River. Its extreme length is nearly 50 miles and it rises to several summits, 2,500 and 3,000 feet high. } Tuskahoma. Poteau. Winding Stair.

Kiamichi; river in Choctaw Nation, a very large left-hand branch of Red River. } Clarkesville. Alikchi. Antlers. Tuskahoma. Winding Stair. Poteau Mountain.

Kickapoo; station on Gulf, Colorado and Santa Fe Railway.

Kickapoo Sandy; creek in Chickasaw Nation, a left-hand branch of Washita River................................... Pauls Valley.

Kill Hollow; valley of Kill Creek, a left-hand branch of Illinois River, a tributary to Arkansas River, in Cherokee Nation... Siloam Springs.

Kings; creek in Choctaw Nation, a very small right-hand branch of Canadian River................................. Tahlequah.

Kings; creek in Choctaw Nation, a right-hand branch of North Boggy Creek, a tributary to Muddy Boggy Creek......... Claremore.

Kingston; post village in Chickasaw Nation................ Denison.

Kinlock; station on St. Louis and San Francisco Railroad.

Kinnison; post village in Cherokee Nation .... Vinita.

Kinta; post village in Choctaw Nation on Fort Smith and Western Railroad.

Kiowa; post village in Choctaw Nation on Missouri, Kansas, and Texas Railway .... McAlester.

Kiowa Hill; summit near Pine Mountain in Choctaw Nation.. McAlester.

Kirks; ferry across Little River in Choctaw Nation........... Lukfata.

Kiser; post village in Chickasaw Nation..................... Pauls Valley.

Kittie; post village in Choctaw Nation.

Klaus; village in Cherokee Nation .... Wyandotte.

Klondike; post village in Chickasaw Nation.

Knox; village in Chickasaw Nation .... Stonewall.

Kosoma; post village in Choctaw Nation on St. Louis and San
Francisco Railroad; elevation, 471 feet.................... Antlers.

Krebs; post village in Choctaw Nation on Choctaw, Oklahoma
and Gulf Railroad .... McAlester.

Kullituklo; post village in Choctaw Nation.

Kullychaha; post village in Choctaw Nation .... Sallisaw.

Lacy; creek in Cherokee Nation, a right-hand branch of Caney
River, a tributary to Verdigris River .... Claremore.

Laflin; creek in Chickasaw Nation, a left-hand branch of {Rush Springs.
Washita River.   {Chickasha.

Lane; post village in Choctaw Nation.

Larue; branch in Cherokee Nation, a left-hand branch of Illinois River, a tributary to Arkansas River .... Muscogee.

Leach; post village in Cherokee Nation .... Siloam Springs.

Leader; creek in Chickasaw and Choctaw nations, a left-hand
branch of Clear Boggy Creek............................ Coalgate.

Leader; village in Choctaw Nation .... Coalgate.

Lebanon; post village in Chickasaw Nation .... Denison.

Lee; creek, a left-hand branch of Arkansas River, heading in {Tahlequah.
Cherokee Nation and flowing into Arkansas.   {Fort Smith.

Lee; post village in Creek Nation.

Lees; spring in Chickasaw Nation .... Stonewall.

Lefore; post village in Choctaw Nation on St. Louis and San
Francisco Railroad.. Winding Stair.

Legal; post village in Choctaw Nation .... Coalgate.

Lehigh; town in Choctaw Nation on Missouri, Kansas and
Texas Railway; population, 1,500; elevation, 936 feet..... Atoka.

Leliaetta; village in Creek Nation on Missouri, Kansas and
Texas Railway; elevation, 589 feet....................... Pryor.

Lenapah; post village in Cherokee Nation on St. Louis, Iron
Mountain and Southern Railway; population, 154; elevation, 759 feet .... Nowata.

Lenna; post village in Creek Nation.

Lenox; village in Choctaw Nation .... Winding Stair.

Lenton; post village in Choctaw Nation.

Leon; post village in Chickasaw Nation; population, 221 ..... Gainesville.

Lester; post village in Chickasaw Nation.

Lick; creek in Chickasaw Nation, a right-hand branch of
Boggy River, a tributary to Red River .... Paris.

Lightning; creek in Cherokee Nation, a left-hand branch of {Nowata.
Verdigris River.   {Vinita.

Limestone; creek in Chickasaw Nation; a right-hand branch
of Blue Creek, a tributary to Blue River .... Stonewall.

Limestone; gap in Limestone Ridge in Choctaw Nation....... McAlester.

Limestone; ridge of Pine Mountains in Choctaw Nation ..... {Tuskahoma.
{Coalgate.
{McAlester.

Limestone Gap; post village near gap of the same name in
Limestone Ridge in Choctaw Nation .... McAlester.

Lindsay; post village in Chickasaw Nation on Chicago, Rock
Island and Pacific Railway.

Line; creek in Chickasaw Nation, a right-hand branch of Washita River .... Chickasha.

Linn; post village in Chickasaw Nation........................ Tishomingo.

Linson; creek in Choctaw Nation, a left-hand branch of Mountain Fork River, a tributary to Little River .... Lukfata.

Linwood; post village in Chickasaw Nation.................. Addington.

Lipe Mound; summit in Cherokee Nation................... Claremore.

Little; post village in Seminole Nation.

Little; river in Choctaw Nation, a large left-hand branch of Red River, rising in Choctaw Nation and flowing south and east into Arkansas, where it discharges into Red River. { Lukfata. Alikchi. Shawneetown.

Little; river in Creek Nation, a left-hand branch of Canadian River. { Stonewall. Coalgate. Wewoka.

Little Blue; river in Choctaw Nation, a right-hand branch of Blue River.. Atoka.

Little Cabin; creek in Cherokee Nation, a left-hand branch of Cabin Creek, a tributary to Neosho River.............. Vinita.

Little California; creek in Cherokee Nation, a left-hand branch of California Creek, a tributary to Verdigris River. Nowata.

Little Cane; creek in Creek Nation, a left-hand branch of Cane Creek, a tributary to Arkansas River .... Okmulgee.

Little Caney; creek in Cherokee Nation, a lelf-hand branch of Caney River, a tributary to Verdigris river .... Nowata.

Little Caney Boggy; creek in Choctaw Nation, a left-hand branch of Clear Boggy Creek .... Coalgate.

Little Catfish; creek in Creek Nation, a left-hand branch of Little Deep Creek, a tributary through Little Deep Fork Creek to Deep Fork of Canadian River.................... Nuyaka.

Little Cedar; creek in Cherokee Nation, a right-hand branch of Clear Creek, a tributary to Neosho River.............. Pryor.

Little Cedar; creek in Choctaw Nation, a left-hand branch of Kiamichi River .... Winding Stair.

Little Cedar; creek in Choctaw Nation, a small left-hand branch of Kiamichi River .... Antlers.

Little Chickasaw; creek in Choctaw Nation, a left-hand branch of Chickasaw Creek, a tributary to Muddy Boggy Creek. { Antlers. Atoka.

Little Deep Fork; creek in Creek Nation, a right-hand branch of Deep Fork of Canadian River.......................... Nuyaka.

Little Dog; creek in Cherokee Nation, a left-hand branch of Dog Creek, a tributary to Verdigris River. { Pryor. Claremore.

Little Eagle; creek in Choctaw Nation, a right-hand branch of Eagle Fork, a tributary to Mountain Fork River .... Winding Stair.

Little East Blue; creek in Chickasaw Nation, a left-hand branch of Blue River. { Tishomingo. Stonewall.

Little Flint; creek in Cherokee Nation, a fork of Flint Creek, a tributary to Illinois River .... Siloam Springs.

Little Fourche Maline; creek in Choctaw Nation, a left-hand branch of Fourche Maline, a tributary to Poteau River.... Tuskahoma.

Little Glasses; creek in Chickasaw Nation, a right-hand branch of Washita River................................. Tishomingo.

Little Greenleaf; creek in Cherokee Nation, a right-hand branch of Greenleaf Creek, a tributary to Arkansas River.. Muscogee.

Little Grief; creek in Creek Nation, a right-hand branch of
Wewoka Creek, a tributary to North Fork of Canadian
River... Wewoka.

Little Hiayona; creek in Chickasaw Nation, a right-hand {Tishomingo.
branch of Hawani Creek, a tributary to Red River.   {Denison.

Little Lee; creek, a right-hand branch of Lee Creek, a tributary to Arkansas River.................................... Tahlequah.

Little Polecat; creek in Creek Nation, a left-hand branch of
Polecat Creek, a tributary to Arkansas River............. Nuyaka.

Little Pryor; creek in Cherokee Nation, a small left-hand {Pryor.
branch of Pryor Creek, a tributary to Neosho River.   {Vinita.

Little Salina; creek in Cherokee Nation, a left-hand branch {Siloam Spring.
of Salina Creek, a tributary to Neosho River.   {Pryor.

Little Sallisaw; creek in Cherokee Nation, a left-hand branch
of Sallisaw Creek, a tributary to Arkansas River .... Sallisaw.

Little Salt; creek in Cherokee Nation, a right-hand branch of {Vinita.
Salt Creek, a tributary to Verdigris River.   {Nowata.

Little Sand; creek in Chickasaw Nation, a left-hand branch
of Sand Creek, a tributary to Red River .... Denison.

Little Sandy; creek in Chickasaw Nation, a left-hand branch
of Blue River .... Tishomingo.

Little Sandy; creek in Chickasaw Nation, a right-hand branch
of Sandy Creek, a tributary to Canadian River .... Stonewall.

Little Sansbois; creek in Choctaw Nation, a right-hand {Sallisaw.
branch of Arkansas River.   {Sansbois.

Little Spring; creek in Cherokee Nation, a right-hand branch
of Spring Creek, a tributary to Neosho River.............. Pryor.

Little Vian; creek in Cherokee Nation, a left-hand branch of {Sallisaw.
Vian Creek, a tributary to Arkansas River.   {Tahlequah.

Little Washita; river in Chickasaw Nation, a right-hand
branch of Washita River................................... Rush Springs.

Little West Blue; creek in Chickasaw Nation, a right-hand {Tishomingo.
branch of Blue River.   {Stonewall.

Little Wewoka; creek in Creek Nation, a left-hand branch of
Wewoka Creek, a tributary to North Fork of Canadian
River.. Wewoka.

Little Wildhorse; creek in Chocktaw Nation, a right-hand
branch of Rock Creek .... Canadian.

Lloyd; post village in Choctaw Nation.

Loco; post village in Chickasaw Nation...................... Addington.

Locust; creek in Cherokee Nation, a left-hand branch of Cabin
Creek, tributary to Neosho River.......................... Vinita.

Locust Grove; post village in Cherokee Nation.............. Pryor.

Lodi; post village in Choctaw Nation.

Lona; village in Choctaw Nation........................... Sansbois.

Lone Grove; post village in Chickasaw Nation; population,
215 .... Ardmore.

Lonelm; post village in Chickasaw Nation.

Long; branch in Choctaw Nation, a right-hand branch of Clear
Boggy Creek .... Atoka.

Long; creek in Choctaw Nation, a right-hand branch of Kia- {Antlers.
michi River, heading in Long Creek and North Fork.   {Alikchi.

Long; creek in Choctaw Nation, a right-hand branch of Fourche ⟨Tuskahoma.
Maline River, a tributary to Poteau River.   ⟨Winding Stair.

Long; post village in Cherokee Nation .... Tahlequah.

Long Branch; creek in Creek Nation, a right-hand branch of
Cosseetta Creek, a tributary to Deep Fork of Canadian River. Okmulgee.

Long George; creek in Creek Nation, a left-hand branch of
Wewoka Creek, a tributary to North Fork of Canadian
River .... Wewoka.

Long Prairie; low stretch of land near the village of Kansas
in Cherokee Nation .... Siloam Springs.

Longtown; creek in Choctaw Nation, a right-hand branch of ⟨Sansbois.
Canadian River.   ⟨Canadian.

Lonloge; lake in Choctaw Nation .... Shawneetown.

Lowrey; post village in Cherokee Nation.

Lowry Prairie; low stretch of land northwest of Illinois River
in Cherokee Nation .... Siloam Springs.

Lucas; village in Cherokee Nation .... Vinita.

Ludlow; post village in Choctaw Nation.

Lukfata; creek in Choctaw Nation, a left-hand branch of Lit-⟨Lukfata.
tle River.   ⟨Shawneetown.

Lukfata; post village in Choctaw Nation .... Shawneetown.

Lula; post village in Choctaw Nation.

Luna; branch in Cherokee Nation, a left-hand branch of Illinois River .... Siloam Springs.

Lutie; post village in Choctaw Nation on Choctaw, Oklahoma
and Gulf Railroad.

Lyceum; village in Choctaw Nation .... Tuskahoma.

Lynn; group of hills in Choctaw Nation south of Kiamichi
Mountains .... Winding Stair.

Lyons; station on Kansas, Missouri and Southern Railway.

McAlester; town in Choctaw Nation on Missouri, Kansas and
Texas Railway; population, 646; elevation, 684 feet....... McAlester.

McCulloch; ferry across Red River in Choctaw Nation........ Shawneetown.

McCurtain; post village in Choctaw Nation on Fort Smith and
Western Railroad.

McDermott; village in Creek Nation .... Wewoka.

McDonald; branch in Cherokee Nation, a left-hand branch of
Cabin Creek, a tributary to Neosho River................. Vinita.

McFall; village in Cherokee Nation.......................... Claremore.

McGee; creek in Choctaw Nation, a left-hand branch of Muddy ⟨McAlester.
Boggy Creek.   ⟨Antlers.

McGee; post village in Chickasaw Nation; population, 209.... Stonewall.

McKennon; creek in Creek Nation, a small intermittent right-
hand branch of Frank Henry Creek, a tributary to Deep
Fork of Canadian River .... Nuyaka.

McKey; post village in Cherokee Nation on St. Louis, Iron
Mountain and Southern Railway .... Sallisaw.

McKinney; creek in Choctaw Nation, a right-hand branch of
Harris Bayou, a tributary to Red River................... Shawneetown.

McKinsey; slough in Choctaw Nation, a backwater from Red
River .... Clarkesville.

McLain; post village in Cherokee Nation..................... Muscogee.

McMillan; post village in Chickasaw Nation.................. Tishomingo.

Mack Chapel; village in Choctaw Nation .... Tuskahoma.

Mackey; station on St. Louis, Iron Mountain and Southern Railway; elevation, 522 feet.

Madden; creek in Cherokee Nation, a right-hand branch of Lightning Creek, a tributary to Verdigris River........... Vinita.

Madill; post village in Choctaw Nation on St. Louis and San Francisco Railroad.

Malhuldy; creek in Choctaw Nation, a right-hand branch of Gaines Creek, a tributary to Canadian River.............. Canadian.

Manard; post village in Cherokee Nation.................... Muscogee.

Mannford; post village in Creek Nation.

Mannsville; post village in Chickasaw Nation on Choctaw, Oklahoma and Gulf Railroad; population, 198............. Tishomingo.

Maple; post village in Cherokee Nation........................ Sallisaw.

Marble; post village in Cherokee Nation on Kansas City Southern Railway .... Tahlequah.

Mariette; post village in Chickasaw Nation on Gulf, Colorado and Santa Fe Railway; population, 842; elevation, 848 feet. Gainesville.

Markham; ferry across Neosho River in Cherokee Nation.

Marlow; post village in Chickasaw Nation on Chicago, Rock Island and Pacific Railway; population, 1,016; elevation, 1,288 feet... Rush Springs.

Marsden; post village in Chickasaw Nation .... Ardmore.

Mass; creek in Chickasaw Nation, a right-hand branch of Wildhorse Creek, a tributary to Washita River. {Pauls Valley. Ardmore.

Massey; post village in Choctaw Nation on Fort Smith and Western Railroad.

Motoaka; station on Atchison, Topeka and Santa Fe Railway.

Matoy; post village in Choctaw Nation.

Maxwell; post village in Chickasaw Nation.................. Stonewall.

Mayhew; village in Choctaw Nation .... Antlers.

Mayhew; creek in Choctaw Nation, a right-hand branch of Clear Boggy Creek .... Antlers.

Maysville; post village in Chickasaw Nation on Gulf, Colorado and Santa Fe Railway.

Mazie; village in Creek Nation on Missouri, Kansas and Texas Railway .... Pryor.

Mead; post village in Chickasaw Nation on St. Louis and San Francisco Railroad .... Denison.

Mekko; station on Missouri, Kansas and Texas Railway.

Melton; lake in the extreme northern part of Cherokee Nation near Verdigris River.............................. Nowata.

Melvin; post village in Cherokee Nation on St. Louis and San Francisco Railroad....................................... Muscogee.

Mekusukey; post villige in Seminole Nation .... Seminole.

Miami; post village in Peoria Reservation on St. Louis and San Francisco Railroad; population, 1,527 .... Wyandotte.

Middle; branch in Cherokee Nation, a right-hand branch of Caney River, a tributary to Verdigris River .... Claremore.

Middle; creek in Creek Nation, a left-hand branch of Canadian River .... Wewoka.

Middle; fork of Cabin Creek, a tributary to Neosho River, in Cherokee Nation .... Vinita.

Midland; post village in Chickasaw Nation.

Midway; post village in Choctaw Nation on Missouri, Kansas and Texas Railway; elevation, 598 feet.

Milburn; post village in Chickasaw Nation on Choctaw, Oklahoma and Gulf Railroad.

Miles; post village in Cherokee Nation .... Vinita.

Mill; creek in Cherokee Nation, a left-hand branch of Cabin Creek, a tributary to Neosho River .... Vinita.

Mill; creek in Chickasaw Nation, a right-hand branch of Clear Boggy Creek .... Stonewall.

Mill; creek in Chickasaw Nation, a left-hand branch of Washita River .... Tishomingo.

Mill; creek in Choctaw Nation, a right-hand branch of North Boggy Creek, a tributary to Muddy Boggy Creek.......... Coalgate.

Mill; creek in Creek Nation, a left-hand branch of Canadian River .... Canadian.

Mill Creek; post village in Chickasaw Nation on St. Louis and San Francisco Railroad .... Tishomingo.

Miller; creek in Creek Nation, a left-hand branch of Verdigris River, a tributary to Arkansas River...................... Claremore.

Milo; post village in Chickasaw Nation.

Milton; post village in Choctaw Nation .... Sallisaw.

Milton; mountain in Choctaw Nation .... Winding Stair.

Mina; post village in Chickasaw Nation.

Minco; post village in Chickasaw Nation on Chicago, Rock Island and Pacific Railway................................ Chickasha.

Mingo; branch in Cherokee and Creek nations, a right-hand branch of Bird Creek, a tributary to Verdigris River..... Claremore.

Mingo; ferry across Verdigris River in Creek Nation .... Muscogee.

Mingo; village in Cherokee Nation on St. Louis and San Francisco Railroad; elevation, 601 feet .... Claremore.

Mintubbe; crescent-shaped lake in the bottom lands of Red River, in Choctaw Nation .... Shawneetown.

Mintubbe; slough in Choctaw Nation, a backwater from Mintubbe Lake,... Shawneetown.

Missouri, Kansas and Texas Railway, having a main line running from Parsons, Kans., southward across the Territory to Denison, with a branch to Oklahoma City and several feeders.

Mitchell; station on St. Louis and San Francisco Railroad.

Modoc; small reservation in the northeastern part of Indian Territory with an area of 6 square miles. The Indians were moved there from northern California. Population, 140; 96 white and 44 Indian .... Wyandotte.

Monk; post village in Chickasaw Nation..................... Ardmore.

Monroe; post village in Choctaw Nation on Choctaw, Oklahoma and Gulf Railroad.................................... Winding Stair.

Monument; creek in Chickasaw Nation, a left-hand branch of Beaver Creek, a tributary to Red River .... Addington.

Monument Hill; summit in Chickasaw Nation.............. Addington.

Montezuma; creek in Creek Nation, a right-hand branch of Deep Fork of Canadian River. { Wewoka. Okmulgee. Nuyaka.

Moodys; post village in Cherokee Nation...................... Siloam Springs.
Moodys; village in Cherokee Nation........................... Tahlequah.
Mormon; creek in Cherokee Nation, a right-hand branch of
    Verdigris River, a tributary to Arkansas River............ Nowata.
Morris; creek in Choctaw Nation, a right-hand branch of Po-
    teau River.. Winding Stair.
Morris; post village in Creek Nation on St. Louis and San
    Francisco Railroad.
Morse; post village in Creek Nation........................... Nuyaka.
Moseley Prairie; level stretch of land north of Illinois River,
    in Cherokee Nation.. Siloam Springs.
Mosely; creek in Cherokee and Choctaw nations, a left-hand
    branch of Delaware Creek, a tributary to Clear Boggy Creek. Atoka.
Mosley; spring in Chickasaw Nation........................... Tishomingo.
Mosquito; creek in Creek Nation, a right-hand branch of Pole-
    cat Creek, a tributary to Arkansas River.................. Nuyaka.
Mossy; creek in Cherokee Nation, an inlet of Big Lake........ Claremore.
Mounds; post village in Creek Nation on St. Louis and San
    Francisco Railroad .... Nuyaka.
Mountain; creek in Chickasaw Nation, a left-hand branch of
    Mud Creek, a tributary to Red River...................... Addington.
Mountain; creek in Choctaw Nation, a right-hand branch of ⎰Winding Stair.
    Poteau River, a tributary to Arkansas River.   ⎱Sallisaw.
Mountain; fork in Choctaw Nation, a left-hand branch of
    Little River, which rises in western Arkansas............. Shawneetown.
Mountain; fork in Choctaw Nation, a right-hand branch of
    Sansbois Creek, a tributary to Arkansas River............ Sansbois.
Mountain; post village in Choctaw Nation .... Sallisaw.

Mountain Fork; river in Choctaw Nation, a large left-hand ⎧Winding Stair.
    branch of Little River.   ⎨Lukfata.
                                                               ⎩Shawneetown.
Mud; creek in Cherokee Nation, a right-hand branch of Neo- ⎰Wyandotte.
    sho River.   ⎱Vinita.
Mud; creek in Cherokee Nation, a small left-hand branch of
    Canadian River .... Sansbois.
Mud; creek in Chickasaw Nation, a left-hand branch of Red ⎰Addington.
    River, heading in East and West Mud creeks.   ⎱Montague.
Mud; creek in Chickasaw Nation, a left-hand branch of Red
    River.. Gainesville.
Mud; creek in Choctaw Nation, a right-hand branch of Little
    River.. Shawneetown.
Muddy Boggy; creek, a left-hand branch of Boggy Creek, ⎧Tishomingo.
    heading in the northwest corner of Choctaw Nation and ⎨Atoka.
    flowing generally southeast to its junction with the Boggy ⎪Antlers.
    Creek.   ⎩Coalgate.
Muldrow; post village in Cherokee Nation on Kansas and Ar-
    kansaw Valley Division of St. Louis, Iron Mountain and
    Southern Railway; population, 465; elevation, 511 feet.... Sallisaw.
Munroe; station on Choctaw, Oklahoma and Gulf Railroad.
Murry; creek in Chickasaw Nation, a right-hand branch of
    Rush Creek, a tributary to Washita River .... Rush Springs.
Murry; crescent-shaped lake in the bottom land of Red River
    in Choctaw Nation .... Shawneetown.

Muscogee; town in Creek Nation on Missouri, Kansas and
Texas Railway. The agency for the Five Civilized Tribes
is located here; population, 4,254; elevation, 600 feet ..... Muscogee.
Muscogee Junction; station on St. Louis and San Francisco
Railroad.
Muse; post village in Choctaw Nation .... Winding Stair.
Muskrat Hollow; valley of Muskrat Creek, a left-hand branch
of Drowning Creek, a tributary to Neosho River, in Chero-
kee Nation .... Siloam Springs.
Muskrat Mountain; summit in Cherokee Nation .... Tahlequah.
Mustang; creek in Cherokee Nation, a left-hand branch of
Cabin Creek, a tributary to Neosho River .... Vinita.
Mute; branch in Choctaw Nation, a right-hand branch of Sans- ⌠Sansbois.
bois Creek, a tributary to Arkansas River.   ⌡Sallisaw.
Nail; creek in Choctaw Nation, a left-hand branch of Poteau ⌠Sallisaw.
River.   ⌡Fort Smith.
Nail; post village in Choctaw Nation on Kansas City Southern
Railway .... Winding Stair.
Naples; post village in Chickasaw Nation .... Chickasha.
Narcissa; post village in Chickasaw Nation on St. Louis and
San Francisco Railroad.
Naudack; post village in Creek Nation.
Nebo; post village in Chickasaw Nation .... Tishomingo.
Needmore; post village in Cherokee Nation.
Negro; creek in Creek Nation, a left-hand branch of Deep Fork ⌠Okmulgee.
of Canadian River.   ⌡Nuyaka.
Negro; fork in Chickasaw Nation, a left-hand branch of Mud
Creek, a tributary to Red River .... Addington.
Nellie Bly; creek in Cherokee Nation, a small right-hand
branch of Double Creek, a tributary to Caney River ...... Nowata.
Nelson; post village in Choctaw Nation .... Antlers.
Neosho; river of Kansas and Indian Territory, a large left-
hand branch of Arkansas River, heading in Kansas a little
east of the center of the State, and flowing first eastward and
then southward to its mouth. Its total length is 346 miles.
Newberry; creek in Chickasaw Nation, a left-hand branch of
Washita River .... Tishomingo.
Newburg; post village in Choctaw Nation.
Newby; post village in Creek Nation.
Newcastle; post village in Chickasaw Nation .... Chickasha.
Newport; post village in Chickasaw Nation .... Ardmore.
New Tishomingo; post village in Chickasaw Nation .... Tishomingo.
Newton; village in Chickasaw Nation .... Stonewall.
Nida; post village in Chickasaw Nation .... Atoka.
Nigger; creek in Cherokee Nation, a left-hand branch of
Arkansas River .... Sallisaw.
Nigger; creek in Choctaw Nation, a right-hand branch of
Brazil Creek, a tributary to Poteau River .... Sallisaw.
Nigger; creek in Creek and Cherokee nations, a right-hand
branch of Neosho River .... Muscogee.
Nigger Sandy; creek in Chickasaw Nation, a left-hand branch
of Washita River .... Pauls Valley.
Ninnekah; post village in Chickasaw Nation on Chicago, Rock
Island and Pacific Railway; elevation, 1,077 feet .... Rush Springs.

Nixon; post village in Choctaw Nation......................... Coalgate.

Nochonohonubbe; creek in Choctaw Nation, a left-hand branch of Little River .... Winding Stair.

Non; post village iu Choctaw Nation.

No Name; creek in Creek Nation, a right-hand branch of Polecat Creek, a tributary to Arkansas River .... Nuyaka.

North; creek in Cherokee Nation, fork of Cotton Creek, a tributary to Caney River................................... Nowata.

North Boggy; creek in Choctaw Nation, a left-hand branch of Muddy Boggy Creek, a tributary to Boggy Creek. { McAlester. Coalgate. Atoka.

North Criner; creek in Chickasaw Nation, a left-hand branch of Criner Creek, a tributary to Washita River .... Chickasha.

North Fork of Canadian; river in Creek Nation, a large left-hand branch of Canadian River. It rises in Oklahoma Territory and flows generally eastward and then south. { Canadian. Wewoka.

North Georges Fork; right-hand branch of Dirty Creek, a tributary to Arkansas River. { Sanbois. Muscogee.

North Jackford; creek in Choctaw Nation, a left-hand branch of Jackford Creek, a tributary to Kiamichi River.......... Tuskahoma.

Norton; ferry across Washita River in Chickasaw Nation..... Tishomingo.

Norton; post village in Chickasaw Nation.

Norwood; creek in Choctaw Nation, a left-hand branch of Red River.. Shawneetown.

Norwood; post village in Choctaw Nation.

Nowata; post village in Cherokee Nation on St. Louis and San Francisco Railroad; population, 498 .... Nowata.

Nowata; station on the St. Louis, Iron Mountain and Southern Railway.

Nuyaka; creek in Creek Nation, a right-hand branch of Deep Fork of Canadian River. { Nuyaka. Wewoka.

Oak Grove; post village in Cherokee Nation.

Oakland; post village in Chickasaw Nation; population, 701.. Tishomingo.

Oak Lodge; post village in Choctaw Nation .... Sallisaw.

Oakman; post village in Chickasaw Nation .... Stonewall.

Oaks; post village in Cherokee Nation .... Siloam Springs.

Oaktaha; station on Missouri, Kansas and Texas Railway.

Oberlin; post village in Chickasaw Nation.................... Paris.

Ochelata; post village in Cherokee Nation on Atchison, Topeka and Santa Fe Railway.

Oconee; post village in Choctaw Nation .... Coalgate.

Octavia; post village in Choctaw Nation.

Odell; post village in Cherokee Nation.

Ogeechee; post village in Cherokee Nation on St. Louis and San Francisco Railroad .... Wyandotte.

Oglesby; post village in Cherokee Nation.

O'Hara; station on St. Louis and San Francisco Railroad.

Oil; creek in Chickasaw Nation, a right-hand branch of Washita River... Tishomingo.

Oil; creek in Chickasaw Nation, a left-hand branch of Washita River... Tishomingo.

Okemah; post village in Creek Nation.

Okfuskee; post village in Creek Nation .... Nuyaka.

Okmulgeᴈ; county seat of Creek Nation on St. Louis and San
  Francisco Railroad .... Okmulgee.
Okmulgee; creek in Creek Nation, a left-hand branch of Adams⌠Okmulgee.
  Creek, a tributary to Deep Fork of Canadian River.   ⌡Nuyaka.
Okmulgee; creek in Creek Nation which sinks in the marsh 2
  miles south of the town of Okmulgee ⸴.................... Okmulgee.
Okoee; post village in Cherokee Nation.
Okra; post village in Chickasaw Nation.
Oktaha; post village in Creek Nation on Missouri, Kansas and
  Texas Railway .... Muscogee.
Old Boggy Creek; village in Choctaw Nation .... Atoka.
Olive; post village in Creek Nation.
Olney; post village in Choctaw Nation on Choctaw, Oklahoma
  and Gulf Railroad.
Olsenville; village in Cherokee Nation...................... Nowata.
One; creek in Choctaw Nation, a right-hand branch of Kiamichi
  River.. Antlers.
Onion; creek in Cherokee Nation, a very small right-hand
  branch of Verdigris River....................⸴............ Nowata.
Oologah; post village in Cherokee Nation on St. Louis, Iron
  Mountain and Southern Railway; population, 308; eleva-
  tion, 655 feet.. Claremore.
Opie; village in Chickasaw Nation .... Addington.
Opossum; creek in Cherokee Nation, a right-hand branch of
  Verdigris River, a tributary to Arkansas River .... Nowata.
Orr; post village in Chickasaw Nation; population, 222 .... Addington.
Osage; creek in Cherokee Nation, a right-hand branch of
  Pryor Creek, a tributary to Neosho River .... Pryor.
Oscar; post village in Chickasaw Nation..................... Montague.
Oseuma; post village in Cherokee Nation on St. Louis and San
  Francisco Railroad; elevation, 814 feet................... Wyandotte.
Oswalt; post village in Chickasaw Nation.
Ottawa; post village in Ottawa Nation.
Ottawa; reservation in the northeastern part of the Territory
  with an area of 23 square miles. Population, 2,205; 2,039
  white, 176 Indian .... Wyandotte.
Otter; creek in Chickasaw Nation, a left-hand branch of Washita
  River... Chickasha.
Otterville; village in Chickasaw Nation .... Ardmore.
Overbrook; post village in Chickasaw Nation on Gulf, Colo-
  rado and Santa Fe Railway; elevation, 733 feet........... Ardmore.
Owasso; post village in Cherokee Nation on Atchison, Topeka
  and Santa Fe Railway.-
Owen; station on Atchison, Topeka and Santa Fe Railway.
Owl; creek in Chickasaw Nation, a left-hand branch of Washita
  River... Pauls Valley.
Owl; creek in Chickasaw Nation, a left-hand branch of Buck
  Creek, a tributary to Clear Boggy Creek . ... Stonewall.
Owl; creek in Chickasaw Nation, a right-hand branch of Hick-
  ory Creek, a tributary to Red River .... Gainesville.
Owl; creek in Choctaw Nation, a left-hand branch of Red River. Clarkesville.
Owl; creek in Choctaw Nation, a left-hand branch of Brazil⌠Sallisaw.
  Creek, a tributary to Poteau River.   ⌡Sansbois.
Owl; creek in Choctaw Nation, a left-hand branch of Leader
  Creek, a tributary to Clear Boggy Creek .... Coalgate.

Owl; post village in Choctaw Nation.

Paden; post village in Creek Nation on Fort Smith and Western Railroad.

Page; post village in Choctaw Nation on Kansas City Southern
Railway .... Winding Stair.

Palmer; post village in Chickasaw Nation .... Stonewall.

Panama; post village in Choctaw Nation on Kansas City
Southern Railway .... Sallisaw.

Panola; village in Choctaw Nation on Choctaw, Oklahoma and
Gulf Railroad; elevation, 623 feet......................... Tuskahoma.

Panther; creek in Cherokee Nation, a left-hand branch of ⎰Vinita.
Lightning Creek, a tributary to Verdigris River. ⎱Nowata.

Panther; creek in Cherokee Nation, a left-hand branch of Verdigris River, a tributary to Arkansas River............... Claremore.

Panther; creek in Chickasaw Nation, a right-hand branch of
Criner Creek, a tributary to Washita River............... Rush Springs.

Panther; creek in Chickasaw Nation, a right-hand branch of
Wildhorse Creek, a tributary to Washita River........... Addington.

Panther; creek in Chickasaw Nation, a right-hand branch of
Rush Creek, a tributary to Washita River................ Pauls Valley.

Panther; creek in Choctaw Nation, a left-hand branch of
Muddy Boggy Creek..................................... Coalgate.

Panther; creek in Creek Nation, a small right-hand branch of
Polecat Creek, a tributary to Arkansas River............ Nuyaka.

Panther; creek in Creek Nation, a right-hand branch of Arkansas River .... Claremore.

Panther; mountain summit in Choctaw Nation .... Sansbois.

Panther; village in Choctaw Nation .... Sallisaw.

Paoli; post village in Chickasaw Nation on Gulf, Colorado and
Santa Fe Railway; population, 234; elevation, 916 feet.... Pauls Valley.

Parkhill; creek in Cherokee Nation, a right-hand branch of
Illinois River .... Tahlequah.

Parkhill; post village in Cherokee Nation on St. Louis and
San Francisco Railroad .... Tahlequah

Parks; post village in Chickasaw Nation.

Paro; post village in Creek Nation.

Parsons; post village in Choctaw Nation.

Pashubbe; creek in Choctaw Nation, a left-hand branch of
Kiamichi River .... Winding Stair.

Patton; village in Choctaw Nation on Missouri, Kansas and
Texas Railway .... Pryor.

Paucaunla; post village in Chickasaw Nation................ Bonham.

Pauls Valley; post village in Chickasaw Nation on Gulf, Colorado and Santa Fe Railway; population, 1,467; elevation,
875 feet .... Pauls Valley.

Pawpaw; creek in Cherokee Nation, a right-hand branch of
Cabin Creek, a tributary to Neosho River................ Vinita.

Pawpaw; post village in Cherokee Nation................... Sallisaw.

Peaceable; creek in Choctaw Nation, a left-hand branch of
Gaines Creek, a tributary to Canadian River .... McAlester.

Peachland; creek in Choctaw Nation, an intermittent right-hand branch of Long Creek, a tributary to Fourche Maline. Tuskahoma.

Peachland Chapel; village in Choctaw Nation .... Tuskahoma.

Pearl; creek in Choctaw Nation, a right-hand branch of Kiamichi River.. Tuskahoma.

Pearl; village in Chickasaw Nation .... Rush Springs.

Peavine; creek in Cherokee Nation, a left-hand branch of Barren Fork, a tributary to Illinois River...................... Tahlequah.

Peavine; creek in Chickasaw Nation, a left-hand branch of Washita River.. Pauls Valley.

Pecan; creek in Cherokee Nation, a right-hand branch of Cedar Creek, a tributary to Neosho River .... Vinita.

Pecan; creek in Choctaw Nation, a right-hand branch of Cache Creek, a tributary to Arkansas River .... Sallisaw.

Pecan; creek in Creek Nation, a right-hand branch of Arkansas River. {Okmulgee. Muscogee.

Peck; post village in Choctaw Nation on Missouri, Kansas and Texas Railway; elevation, 615 feet.

Peggs; post village in Cherokee Nation.

Pennington; creek in Chickasaw Nation, a left-hand branch of Washita River .... Tishomingo.

Peno; station on Kansas City Southern Railway.

Pensacola; post village in Cherokee Nation .... Pryor.

Peoria; post village in Peoria Reservation; population, 144... Wyandotte.

Peoria; reservation in the northeastern part of Territory with an area of 79 square miles. Population, 1,180; 995 white, 184 Indian .... Wyandotte.

Pero; creek, a left-hand branch of Little River, rising in Choctaw Nation and flowing into Little River in Arkansas. Lukfata.

Perry; creek in Choctaw Nation, a left-hand branch of Red River.. Shawneetown.

Perry; village in Choctaw Nation on Kansas City Southern Railway; elevation, 660 feet............................... Winding Stair.

Perryville; creek in Choctaw Nation, a right-hand branch of Peaceable Creek, a tributary to Gaines Creek.............. McAlester.

Peter Sandy; creek in Chickasaw Nation, a left-hand branch of Blue River .... Tishomingo.

Petersburg; post village in Chickasaw Nation................ Montague.

Petros; village in Choctaw Nation, on Kansas City Southern Railway .... Winding Stair.

Philadelphia; creek in Creek Nation, a right-hand branch of Nuyaka Creek, a tributary to Deep Fork of Canadian River. {Nuyaka. Wewoka.

Philipsburg; village in Creek Nation .... Nuyaka.

Phillips; post village in Choctaw Nation on Missouri, Kansas and Texas Railway .... Coalgate.

Phillips; mountains in Choctaw Nation..................... Winding Stair.

Pickens; village in Chickasaw Nation....................... Tishomingo.

Pickwick; station on St. Louis and San Francisco Railroad.

Pigeon; creek in Choctaw Nation, a right-hand branch of Kiamichi River .... Winding Stair.

Pike; post village in Chickasaw Nation...................... Gainesville.

Pine; creek in Cherokee Nation, a left-hand branch of Vine Creek, a tributary to Arkansas River..................... Tahlequah.

Pine; creek in Chickasaw Nation, a right-hand branch of Mud Creek, a tributary to Red River .... Addington.

Pine; creek in Choctaw Nation, a right-hand branch to Little River....... .... Alikchi.

Pine; creek in Choctaw Nation, a left-hand branch of Kiamichi River. {McAlester. Antlers.

Pine; mountains, a name applied to some disconnected, broken ridges of the Ozark Hills in Choctaw Nation, trending generally northeast and southwest.
{ Wyandotte.
Lukfata.
McAlester.
Coalgate.
Tuskahoma.

Pine; post village in Choctaw Nation.

Piney; creek in Choctaw Nation, a left-hand branch of Caney Boggy Creek, a tributary to Muddy Boggy Creek .... Coalgate.

Piney; creek in Choctaw Nation, a right-hand branch of Longtown Creek, a tributary to Canadian River .... Sansbois.

Platter; post village in Chickasaw Nation.

Platter Junction; station on St. Louis and San Francisco Railroad.

Plumb; creek in Cherokee Nation, a left-hand branch of Verdigris River, a tributary to Arkansas River. { Vinita.
Nowata.

Pocahontas; village in Choctaw Nation on St. Louis and San Francisco Railroad; elevation, 556 feet.................... Winding Stair.

Pocasset; post village in Chickasaw Nation.

Pocola; post village in Choctaw Nation...................... Sallisaw.

Poindexter; ferry across Neosho River in Cherokee Nation... Pryor.

Pointer; creek in Choctaw Nation, a right-hand branch of Boggy Creek .... Antlers.

Poison; station on Missouri, Kansas and Texas Railway.

Polecat; creek in Creek Nation, a right-hand branch of Arkansas River. { Nuyaka.
Claremore.

Pond; creek in Chickasaw Nation, a right-hand branch of Canadian River .... Chickasha.

Pontotoc; post village in Chickasaw Nation; population, 366.. Tishomingo.

Porter; post village in Creek Nation on Missouri, Kansas and Texas Railway.

Porum; village in Cherokee Nation .... Sansbois.

Posey; creek in Creek Nation, a right-hand branch of Arkansas River .... Okmulgee.

Posey; village in Creek Nation .... Okmulgee.

Possum; creek in Choctaw Nation, a right-hand branch of Brazil Creek, a tributary to Poteau River .... Sallisaw.

Possum; creek in Choctaw Nation, a left-hand branch of Kiamichi River.. Alikchi.

Possum; creek in Creek Nation, a right-hand branch of North Fork of Canadian River, tributary to Canadian River..... Canadian.

Postoak; creek in Cherokee Nation, a left-hand branch of Caney River, a tributary to Verdigris River............... Nowata.

Postoak; creek in Chickasaw Nation, a left-hand branch of Mud Creek, a tributary to Red River .... Addington.

Potato; creek in Choctaw Nation, a right-hand branch of McGee Creek, a tributary to Muddy Boggy Creek .... Antlers.

Potato; group of hills in Choctaw Nation.................... Winding Stair.

Potato; summits in Choctaw Nation .... Sallisaw.

Poteau; post village in Choctaw Nation on Kansas City Southern Railway; population 1,182; elevation, 484 feet .... Sallisaw.

Poteau; ridge of the Ozark Hills north of Poteau River, lying mainly in Arkansas and extends but slightly into Choctaw Nation. The greatest altitude is about 2,500 feet.......... Winding Stair.

Poteau; river, a large right-hand branch of Arkansas River, heading in Arkansas and flowing through Choctaw Nation.
Fort Smith.
Sallisaw.
Winding Stair.
Poteau Mt.

Powell; post village in Chickasaw Nation .... Denison.

Prairie Center; village in Cherokee Nation; elevation, 778 feet .... Vinita.

Praper; post village in Creek Nation.

Price; post village in Creek Nation.

Proctor; post village in Cherokee Nation on St. Louis and San Francisco Railroad.

Proctor; village in Creek Nation........................... Canadian.

Provence; post village in Chickasaw Nation on Choctaw, Oklahoma and Gulf and St. Louis and San Francisco railroads... Ardmore.

Pryor; creek in Cherokee Nation, a right-hand branch of Neosho River.
Vinita.
Pryor.

Pryor Creek; post village in Cherokee Nation on Missouri, Kansas and Texas Railway; population, 495; elevation, 625 feet... Pryor.

Pumpkin; creek in Chickasaw Nation, a left-hand branch of Hickory Creek, a tributary to Red River .... Ardmore.

Purcell; town in Chickasaw Nation on the south bank of Canadian River on Gulf, Colorado and Santa Fe Railway; population, 2,277; elevation, 1,027 feet.

Purdy; post village in Chickasaw Nation; population, 250 .... Rush Springs.

Purgatory; creek in Cherokee Nation, a left-hand branch of Caney River, a tributary to Verdigris River.............. Nowata.

Quapaw; post village in Quapaw Reservation on St. Louis and San Francisco Railroad.

Quapaw; reservation in the northeastern part of the Territory with an area of 89 square miles. Population, 800; 611 white and 189 Indian................................. .. Wyandotte.

Quentin; peak in Rich Mountains in Choctaw Nation........ Winding Stair.

Quinton; post village in Choctaw Nation on Fort Smith and Western Railroad.

Rabb; creek in Cherokee Nation, a left-hand branch of Caney River, a tributary to Verdigris River.
Nowata.
Claremore.

Rain; creek in Choctaw Nation, a right-hand branch of Little River.. Alikchi.

Rainey; station on St. Louis and San Francisco Railroad.

Ramona; station on Atchison, Topeka and Santa Fe Railway.

Ran; post village in Chickasaw Nation .... Tishomingo.

Randolph; post village in Chickasaw Nation on Choctaw, Oklahoma and Gulf and St. Louis and San Francisco railroads.

Rattlesnake; creek in Cherokee Nation, right-hand branch of Spavinaw Creek.. Siloam Springs.

Rattlesnake; mountains ridge in Cherokee Nation ....
Muscogee.
Sansbois.

Ravia; post village in Chickasaw Nation on St. Louis and San Francisco Railroad; population, 128..................... Tishomingo.

Raysville; village in Chickasaw Nation .... Tishomingo.

Rea; station on Choctaw, Oklahoma and Gulf Railroad.

Reagan; post village in Chickasaw Nation...................... Tishomingo.

Reams; village in Choctaw Nation on Missouri, Kansas and
   Texas Railway; elevation, 612 feet......................... Canadian.

Reck; post village in Chickasaw Nation .... Ardmore.

Red; branch in Chickasaw Nation, a right-hand branch of
   Washita River... Pauls Valley.

Red; creek in Chickasaw Nation, a left-hand branch of Red ⌠Addington.
   River.   ⌡Montague.

Red; lake in Choctaw Nation, a crescent-shaped cut-off from
   Red River... Shawneetown.

Red; lake in Choctaw Nation .... Clarkesville.

Red; river of Texas, Oklahoma, Indian Territory, Arkansas,
   and Louisiana. A large western branch of Mississippi
   River heading in the Staked Plains and flowing with a
   course a little south of east, turning to southeast at the
   southeast corner of Indian Territory and entering Mississippi River near the middle of the State of Louisiana. ⌐ Gainesville.
   For several hundred miles it is the boundary between   Denison.
   Oklahoma and Indian Territory on the north and Texas
   on the south. The length of Red River is somewhat in
   excess of 1,000 miles and the area of its drainage basin
   89,970 square miles.

Redbank; creek in Choctaw Nation, a right-hand branch of
   Cache Creek, a tributary to Arkansas River.............. Sallisaw.

Redbird; post village in Creek Nation.

Redden; post village in Choctaw Nation.

Redfork; post village in Creek Nation on St. Louis and San
   Francisco Railroad; elevation, 669 feet.

Redland; post village in Cherokee Nation on Kansas City
   Southern Railway.. Sallisaw.

Redoak; post village in Choctaw Nation on Choctaw, Oklahoma and Gulf Railroad; elevation, 586 feet.............. Tuskahoma.

Redoak; summit in Choctaw Nation........................ Tuskahoma.

Redwood; station on St. Louis and San Francisco Railroad.

Rego; small town in Choctaw Nation....................... Winding Stair.

Reichert; post village in Choctaw Nation .... Winding Stair.

Remy; post village in Cherokee Nation .... Sallisaw.

Rex; post village in Cherokee Nation.

Reynolds; post village in Choctaw Nation on Missouri, Kansas and Texas and Choctaw, Oklahoma and Gulf railroads.. McAlester.

Rice; creek in Cherokee Nation, a left-hand branch of Caney
   River, a tributary to Verdigris River .... Nowata.

Rich; mountains, a ridge of the Ozark Hills in Arkansas and ⌐Winding Stair.
   Choctaw Nation, trending generally east and west, with an │Poteau Mountains.
   altitude slightly exceeding 3,500 feet.   ⌡

Ridge; post village in Creek Nation.

Ringo; village in Cherokee Nation......................... Nowata.

Ritter; creek in Choctaw Nation, a left-hand branch of Blue
   River... Atoka.

Roaring; creek in Chickasaw Nation, a right-hand branch of
   Washita River, heading in Middle and East Roaring creeks. Rush Springs.

Robbers Roost; post village in Chickasaw Nation .... Atoka.

Robberson; post village in Chickasaw Nation .... Rush Springs.

Robbins; post village in Creek Nation.

Roberta; post village in Choctaw Nation .... Bonham.

Roberts; post village in Choctaw Nation.

Robuck; lake in Choctaw Nation .... Paris.

Rock; branch in Cherokee Nation, a left-hand branch of Illinois River .... Siloam Springs.

Rock; branch in Choctaw Nation, a left-hand branch of Blue River, a tributary to Red River........................... Atoka.

Rock; creek in Cherokee Nation, a right-hand branch of Neosho River .... Pryor.

Rock; creek in Chickasaw Nation, a left-hand branch of Clear Boggy Creek .... Coalgate.

Rock; creek in Chickasaw Nation, a left-hand branch of Walnut Bayou, a tributary to Red River .... Gainesville.

Rock; creek in Chickasaw Nation, a left-hand branch of Washita River .... Tishomingo.

Rock; creek in Chickasaw Nation, a left-hand branch of Washita River, heading in South Fork.
{ Ardmore.
Tishomingo.
Stonewall.

Rock; creek in Chickasaw Nation, a left-hand branch of Washita River .... Tishomingo.

Rock; creek in Chickasaw Nation, a left-hand branch of Wildhorse Creek, a tributary to Washita River................. Pauls Valley.

Rock; creek in Chickasaw Nation, a right-hand branch of Canadian River .... Stonewall.

Rock; creek in Chickasaw Nation, a left-hand branch of Washita River, a tributary to Red River...................... Denison.

Rock; creek in Chickasaw Nation, a left-hand branch of Red River... Denison.

Rock; creek in Choctaw Nation, a left-hand branch of Caney Boggy Creek, a tributary to Muddy Boggy Creek.......... Coalgate.

Rock; creek in Choctaw Nation, a right-hand branch of Muddy Boggy Creek .... Coalgate.

Rock; creek in Choctaw Nation, a left-hand branch of Kiamichi River... Tuskahoma.

Rock; creek, in Choctaw Nation, a left-hand branch of Brazil Creek, a tributary to Poteau River.
{ Tuskahoma.
Sansbois.

Rock; creek in Choctaw Nation; a right-hand branch of Possum Creek, a tributary to Kiamichi River................. Alikchi.

Rock; creek in Chocktaw Nation, a left-hand branch of Salt Creek, a tributary to Clear Boggy Creek................... Atoka.

Rock; creek in Choctaw Nation, a right-hand branch of Mountain Fork River .... Lukfata.

Rock; creek in Chocktaw Nation, a left-hand branch of Little River, heading in Choctaw Nation and flowing into Arkansas... Lukfata.

Rock; creek in Choctaw Nation, a left-hand branch of Gaines Creek, a tributary to Canadian River .... Canadian.

Rock; creek in Creek Nation, a left-hand branch of Little Deep Fork Creek, a tributary to Deep Fork River.............. Nuyaka.

Rock; creek in Creek Nation, a right-hand branch of Arkansas River... Nuyaka.

Rock; creek in Creek Nation, a right-hand branch of North Fork of Canadian River................................... Wewoka.

Rock Chimney; ferry across Kiamichi River in Choctaw Nation.. Alikchi.

Rocky; branch in Chickasaw Nation, a small left-hand branch of Rock Creek, a tributary to Washita River .... Tishomingo.

Rodney; village in Choctaw Nation, on St. Louis and San Francisco Railroad; elevation, 471 feet................... Antlers.

Rodtky; creek in Chickasaw Nation, a right-hand branch of Sandy Creek, a tributary to Canadian River.............. Stonewall.

Roff; post village in Chickasaw Nation on St. Louis and San Francisco Railroad .... Stonewall.

Rogers; station on Missouri, Kansas and Texas Railway.

Rose; post village in Cherokee Nation .... Pryor.

Rose Hill; village in Choctaw Nation........................ Clarkesville.

Ross; creek in Choctaw Nation, a left-hand branch of Red River.. Shawneetown.

Ross; station on St. Louis, Iron Mountain and Southern Railway; elevation, 608 feet.

Round; creek in Chickasaw Nation, a right-hand branch of Washita River .... Rush Springs.

Round; mountain ridge in Choctaw Nation, a part of Kiamichi Mountains. {Poteau Mountain. / Winding Stair.

Rowland; station on St. Louis, Iron Mountain and Southern Railway.

Rubottom; post village in Chickasaw Nation.

Ruby; post village in Cherokee Nation....................... Vinita.

Rud; post village in Chickasaw Nation.

Rules; ferry across Red River in Choctaw Nation............ Shawneetown.

Rush; creek in Chickasaw Nation, a right-hand branch of Washita River .... Pauls Valley.

Rush Springs; town in Chickasaw Nation on Chicago, Rock Island and Pacific Railway; elevation, 1,288 feet; population, 518.. Rush Springs.

Russell; creek in Cherokee Nation, a right-hand branch of Neosho River .... Vinita.

Russel Creek; station on Missouri, Kansas and Texas Railway; elevation, 862 feet.

Russelville; post village in Choctaw Nation.................. Sansbois.

Russet; post village in Chickasaw Nation on Choctaw, Oklahoma and Gulf Railroad .... Tishomingo.

Ryan; post village in Chickasaw Nation, on Chicago, Rock Island and Pacific Railway..................................... Addington.

Sacras; ferry across Red River in Chickasaw Nation.......... Ardmore.

Sageeyah; post village in Cherokee Nation; elevation, 644 feet. Claremore.

Sager; creek in Cherokee Nation, a fork of Flint Creek, a tributary to Illinois River .... Siloam Springs.

St. Louis and San Francisco Railroad; an extensive system with several lines traversing the Territory in various directions; one crosses the Territory in a southwestern direction from Pierre City, Mo., to Lawton, Okla.; another from Sapulpa on this line southward to Denison, Tex.; another from Fort Smith, Ark., southward to Paris, Tex., crossing the southeastern part of the Territory; another from Fayetteville, Ark., to Okmulgee; and, finally, a line in the southern part of the Territory from Hope, Ark., to Ardmore.

St. Louis, Iron Mountain and Southern Railway; there is but one line of this extensive system in the Territory, running from Coffeeville, in the eastern part of Kansas, southward and eastward to Fort Smith, Ark.

Salali; creek in Cherokee Nation, a right-hand branch of Bird Creek, a tributary to Verdigris River.............. Claremore.

Salem Springs; village in Cherokee Nation on Barren Fork.. Tahlequah.

Salina; creek in Cherokee Nation, a left-hand branch of Neosho River, a tributary to Arkansas River...................... Siloam Springs.

Salina; post village in Cherokee Nation...................... Pryor.

Saline; village in Choctaw Nation .... Pryor.

Sallisaw; creek in Cherokee Nation, a left-hand branch of{Sallisaw.
Arkansas River.   {Tahlequah.

Sallisaw; post village in Cherokee Nation on St. Louis, Iron Mountain and Southern and Kansas City Southern railways; population, 965; elevation, 530 feet...................... Sallisaw.

Salt; creek in Cherokee Nation, a small right-hand branch of Little Lee Creek, a tributary to Arkansas River .... Tahlequah.

Salt; creek in Cherokee Nation, a left-hand branch of Verdi-{Nowata.
gris River, a tributary to Arkansas River.   {Vinita.

Salt; creek in Chickasaw Nation, a left-hand branch of Washita River, heading in North and South forks.............. Chickasha.

Salt; creek in Chickasaw Nation, a small right-hand branch{Gainesville.
of Hickory Creek, a tributary to Red River.   {Denison.

Salt; creek in Chickasaw Nation, a left-hand branch of Wild-{Pauls Valley.
horse Creek, a tributary to Washita River.   {Rush Springs.

Salt; creek in Choctaw Nation, a right-hand branch of Clear Boggy Creek .... Atoka.

Salt; creek in Creek Nation, a left-hand branch of Deep Fork of Canadian River....................................... Nuyaka.

Salt; creek in Creek Nation, a right-hand branch of Deep Fork of Canadian River.................................. Nuyaka.

Salt; creek in Creek Nation, a left-hand branch of Bad Creek, a tributary to North Fork of Canadian River .... Wewoka.

Salt; creek, a right-hand branch of Shawnee Creek, a tributary to Canadian River....................................... Coalgate.

Salt; creek in Seminole Nation, a right-hand branch of Little River, a tributary to Canadian River .... Seminole.

Salter; creek in Choctaw Nation, a right-hand branch of Kiamichi River.. Alikchi.

Sam; creek in Creek and Cherokee nations, a right-hand branch of Coata Creek, a tributary to Arkansas River..... Muscogee.

Sam; post village in Choctaw Nation.

Sam Lee; station on Chicago, Rock Island and Pacific Railway.

Sand; branch in Chickasaw Nation, a right-hand branch of Caddo Creek, a tributary to Washita River............:..... Ardmore.

Sand; creek in Cherokee Nation, a right-hand branch of Caney River, a tributary to Verdigris River...................... Nowata.

Sand; creek in Chickasaw Nation, a left-hand branch of Red River... Denison.

Sand; creek in Chickasaw Nation, a right-hand branch of Rock Creek, a tributary to Red River .... Denison.

Sand; creek in Chickasaw Nation, a right-hand branch of Caddo Creek, a tributary to Washita River............... Ardmore.

Sand; creek in Chickasaw Nation, a left-hand branch of Washita
River... Tishomingo.
Sand; creek in Choctaw Nation, a left-hand branch of Muddy
Boggy Creek... Coalgate.
Sand; creek in Choctaw Nation, a right-hand branch of Big
Creek, a tributary to Canadian River...................... Coalgate.
Sand; creek in Choctaw Nation, a right-hand branch of Muddy
Boggy Creek.. Atoka.
Sand; creek in Creek Nation, a left-hand branch of Little Deep
Fork Creek, a tributary to Deep Fork River.............. Nuyaka.
Sand; creek in Seminole Nation, a left-hand branch of North
Fork of Canadian River.................................. Seminole.
Sandy; creek in Chickasaw Nation, a left-hand branch of Wild-
horse Creek, a tributary to Washita River................. Pauls Valley.
Sandy; creek in Chickasaw Nation, a right-hand branch of
Rock Creek, a tributary to Washita River.................. Ardmore.
Sandy; creek in Chickasaw Nation, a right-hand branch of
Canadian River .... Stonewall.
Sandy; creek in Chickasaw Nation, a right-hand branch of Big
Sandy Creek, tributary to Washita River .... Tishomingo.
Sandy; creek in Choctaw Nation, a right-hand branch of Clear ⎰Atoka.
Boggy Creek.   ⎱Tishomingo.
Sandy; creek in Choctaw and Chickasaw nations, a left-hand
branch of Blue River..................................... Atoka.
Sandy; creek in Choctaw Nation, a right-hand branch of Dela-
ware Creek, a tributary to Clear Boggy Creek .... Atoka.
Sandy; creek in Choctaw Nation, a left-hand branch of Clear
Boggy Creek... Atoka.
Sandy; creek in Choctaw Nation, a left-hand branch of Coal ⎰Coalgate.
Creek, a tributary to Gaines Creek.   ⎱McAlester.
Sandy; creek in Creek Nation, a left-hand branch of Deep
Fork of Canadian River, heading in East and West forks . Nuyaka.
Sandy Bear; creek in Chickasaw Nation, a left-hand branch of⎰Rush Springs.
Wildhorse Creek, a tributary to Washita River.   ⎱Addington.
Sandstone; ridge in Choctaw Nation........................ Antlers.
Sandtown; village in Cherokee Nation...................... Sallisaw.
Sansbois; creek in Choctaw Nation, a right-hand branch of ⎰Sallisaw.
Arkansas River.   ´   ⎱Sansbois.
Sansbois; group of hills in Choctaw Nation with an altitude
slightly exceeding 1,550 feet............................. Sallisaw.
Sansbois; post village in Choctaw Nation .... Sansbois.
Santa Rosa; village in Seminole Nation...................... Seminole.
Sapulpa; post village in Creek Nation on St. Louis and San
Francisco Railroad; population, 891; elevation, 718 feet... Nuyaka.
Sasakwa; post village in Seminole Nation on St. Louis and
San Francisco Railroad .... Stonewall.
Sassafras; creek in Choctaw Nation, a left-hand branch of
Island Bayou, a tributary to Red River................... Bonham.
Saunders; creek in Cherokee Nation, a right-hand branch of
Caney River, a tributary to Verdigris River.............. Claremore.
Saunders; creek in Cherokee Nation, a right-hand branch of
Holly Creek, a tributary to Neosho River................. Wyandotte.
Savanna; post village in Choctaw Nation on Missouri, Kansas
and Texas Railway; elevation, 724 feet .... McAlester.

Sawokla, post village in Creek Nation.

Sawyer; post village in Choctaw Nation.

Saylor; post village in Choctaw Nation.

Scaly Bark Mountain; summit in Cherokee Nation .... Pryor.

Schoolhouse; creek in Cherokee Nation, a left-hand branch of
　Canadian River .... Sansbois.

Schulter; post village in Creek Nation on St. Louis and San
　Francisco Railroad.

Scipio; post village in Choctaw Nation .... Canadian.

Scipio; creek in Choctaw Nation, a right-hand branch of Cana-⎰Canadian.
　dian River. ⎱Wewoka.

Scullin; station on St. Louis and San Francisco Railroad.

Sealy; station on St. Louis and San Francisco Railroad.

Seef; summit in Rich Mountains in Choctaw Nation.......... Winding Stair.

Seminole; creek in Cherokee Nation, a right-hand branch of
　Pryor Creek, a tributary to Neosho River................. Pryor.

Seminole; station on St. Louis, Iron Mountain and Southern
　Railway; elevation, 731 feet.

Seminole Nation; reservtion with an area of 312 square miles.
　Its surface is rolling and well imbered with post oak and
　black-jack. The capital is Wewoka. Population, 3,790;
　1,143 white, 981 negro, and 1,662 Indian.

Seneca; reservation in the northeastern part of the Territory
　with an area of 81 square miles. Population, 970; 799
　white and 171 Indian .... Wyandotte.

Senora; post village in Creek Nation.

Sequoya; village in Cherokee Nation on St. Louis and San
　Francisco Railroad; elevation, 692 feet.................... Claremore.

Shady Point; post village in Choctaw Nation on Kansas City
　Southern Railway... Salisaw.

Shakespeare; post village in Cherokee Nation.

Sharp; post village in Creek Nation.

Shawnee; reservation in the northeastern part of the Territory
　with an area of 20 square miles. Population, 297; 239
　white and 58 Indian .... Wyandotte.

Shawnee; creek in Cherokee Nation, a left-hand branch of
　Cabin Creek, a tributary to Neosho River................. Vinita.

Shawnee; creek in Choctaw Nation, a right-hand branch of
　Canadian River .... Coalgate.

Shawnee; ridge of hills in Choctaw Nation................... Coalgate.

Shawneetown; post village in Choctaw Nation .... Shawneetown.

Shay; post village in Chickasaw Nation.

Sheep; creek in Chickasaw Nation, a right-hand branch of
　Clear Boggy Creek .... Stonewall.

Shiggin; creek in Chickasaw Nation, a right-hand branch of
　Hickory Creek, a tributary to Red River .... Gainesville.

Short; mountain in Choctaw Nation .... Sallisaw.

Silo; post village in Chickasaw Nation; population, 246....... Atoka.

Simon; creek in Chickasaw Nation, a right-hand branch of ⎰Ardmore.
　Walnut Bayou, a tributary to Red River. ⎱Gainesville.

Simon; creek in Choctaw Nation, a left-hand branch of Blue
　River.. Atoka.

Simon; post village in Chickasaw Nation.................... Ardmore.

Simpson; village in Chickasaw Nation .... Tishomingo.
Simpson; village in Choctaw Nation .... McAlester.
Sincere; creek in Choctaw and Chickasaw nations, a right-hand {Coalgate.
branch of Muddy Boggy Creek.   {Stonewall.
Sixkiller; ferry across Neosho River in Cherokee Nation...... Pryor.
Sixmile; creek in Chickasaw Nation, a left-hand branch of
Rock Creek, a tributary to Washita River................. Tishomingo.
Sixmile; creek in Choctaw Nation, a left-hand branch of
Mountain Fork River, a tributary to Little River......... Lukfata.
Skiatook; post village in Cherokee Nation................... Claremore.
Skin Bayou; branch in Cherokee Nation, a left-hand branch {Sallisaw.
of Arkansas River.   {Tahlequah.
Skull; creek in Creek Nation, a left-hand branch of Little Deep
Fork Creek, a tributary to Deep Fork of Canadian River.. Nuyaka.
Smallwood; station on Missouri, Kansas and Texas Railway.
Smithville; post village in Choctaw Nation.................. Lukfata.
Snail; creek in Cherokee Nation, a left-hand branch of Holly
Creek, a tributary to Neosho River....................... Wyandotte.
Snake; creek in Cherokee Nation, a right-hand branch of
Pryor Creek, a tributary to Neosho River................. Vinita.
Snake; creek in Choctaw Nation, a small right-hand branch of
Canadian River .... Sansbois.
Snake; creek in Creek Nation, a right-hand branch of Arkansas
River.. Okmulgee.
Snake; mountain in Cherokee Nation....................... Tahlequah.
Sneed; post village in Chickasaw Nation.
Snow; creek in Cherokee Nation, a left-hand branch of Verdi- {Vinita.
gris River, a tributary to Arkansas River.   {Nowata.
Sofka; village in Creek Nation............................. Nuyaka.
Soldier; creek in Chickasaw Nation, a right-hand branch of
Washita River .... Rush Springs.
Soper; post village in Choctaw Nation on St. Louis and San
Francisco Railroad.
South Canadian; village in Choctaw Nation on Missouri,
Kansas and Texas Railway; elevation, 660 feet........... Canadian.
South Fork; branch in Cherokee Nation, a right-hand branch
of Dirty Creek, a tributary to Arkansas River .... Sansbois.
South McAlester; town of Choctaw Nation on Missouri,
Kansas and Texas and Choctaw, Oklahoma and Gulf rail-
roads; population, 3,479; elevation, 716 feet.............. McAlester.
Sowder; post village in Cherokee Nation.
Spaniard; creek in Cherokee Nation, a right-hand branch of
Arkansas River.. Muscogee.
Spaulding; post village in Creek Nation on St. Louis and San
Francisco Railroad.
Spavinaw; creek in Cherokee Nation, a left-hand branch of {Siloam Springs.
Neosho River, a tributary to Arkansas River.   {Pryor.
Spavinaw; post village in Cherokee Nation .... Pryor.
Spencer; left-hand branch of Verdigris River, a tributary to {Nowata.
Arkansas River.   {Vinita.
Spencer; creek in Choctaw Nation, a left-hand branch of Kia-
michi River.. Alikchi.
Spencerville; post village in Choctaw Nation.

Sperry; post village in Cherokee Nation.

Spiro; post village in Choctaw Nation on Kansas City Southern Railway; population, 543 .... Sallisaw.

Spokogee; post village in Creek Nation on Fort Smith and Western Railroad.

Spring; branch in Chickasaw Nation, a right-hand branch of Hickory Creek, a tributary to Red River................. Ardmore.

Spring; branch in Creek Nation, a left-hand branch of Canadian River.   {Coalgate. | Wewoka.

Spring; creek in Cherokee Nation, a left-hand branch of Neosho River.   {Siloam Springs. | Pryor.

Spring; creek in Chickasaw Nation, a left-hand branch of Pennington Creek, a tributary to Washita River .... Tishomingo.

Spring; creek in Chickasaw Nation, a left-hand branch of Caddo Creek, a tributary to Washita River............... Ardmore.

Spring; creek in Chickasaw Nation, a left-hand branch of Bitter Creek, a tributary to Washita River.................. Chickasha.

Spring; creek in Chickasaw Nation, a left-hand branch of Rock Spring Creek, a tributary to Washita River......... Pauls Valley.

Spring; creek in Chickasaw Nation, a left-hand branch of Sandy Creek, a tributary to Canadian River.............. Stonewall.

Spring; creek in Chickasaw Nation, a left-hand branch of Sandy Creek, a tributary to Canadian River.............. Stonewall.

Spring; creek in Choctaw Nation, a right-hand branch of Canadian River.. Coalgate.

Springer; post village in Chickasaw Nation .... Ardmore.

Spunky; branch in Creek and Cherokee nations, a right-hand branch of Verdigris River............................... Claremore.

Stanley; a small village in Choctaw Nation on St. Louis and San Francisco Railroad .... Tuskahoma.

Starr; post village in Choctaw Nation....................... Sallisaw.

Starr Hollow; valley of Starr Creek, an intermittent left-hand branch of Falls Branch, a tributary to Illinois River, in Cherokee Nation .... Siloam Springs.

Starvilla; post village in Cherokee Nation .... Sansbois.

Sterrett; post village in Choctaw Nation on Missouri, Kansas and Texas Railway; population, 575...................... Bonham.

Stick; branch in Cherokee Nation, a left-hand branch of Caney River, a tributary to Verdigris River .... Nowata.

Stidham; creek in Creek Nation, a right-hand branch of North Fork of Canadian River.................................. Wewoka.

Stidham; post village in Creek Nation.

Stigler; post village in Choctaw Nation .... Sansbois.

Stilwell; post village in Cherokee Nation on Kansas City Southern Railway; population, 779 .... Tahlequah.

Stonebluff; post village in Creek Nation.

Stonewall; post village in Chickasaw Nation .... Stonewall.

Story; post village in Chickasaw Nation .... Pauls Valley.

Strawberry; creek in Creek Nation, a right-hand branch of Verdigris River, a tributary to Arkansas River.   {Okmulgee. | Muscogee.

Stringtown; post village in Choctaw Nation on Missouri, Kansas and Texas Railway; elevation, 623 feet............... Atoka.

Stuart; post village in Choctaw Nation on Choctaw, Oklahoma and Gulf Railroad; elevation, 722 feet.................... Coalgate.

Suagee; village in Cherokee Nation......................... Wyandotte.

Sugar; creek in Choctaw Nation, a left-hand branch of Boggy
 Creek .... Antlers.
Sugar; creek in Choctaw Nation, a left-hand branch of Poteau
 River .... Winding Stair.
Sugar; mountain in Cherokee Nation .... Tahlequah.
Sugarloaf; creek in Choctaw Nation, a small left-hand branch ⎰Winding Stair.
 of Poteau River.   ⎱Sallisaw.
Sugarloaf; mountain in Choctaw Nation; elevation, 2,600 feet. Atoka.
Sugarloaf; ridge of mountains in Choctaw Nation extending
 into Arkansas.. Sallisaw.
Sugden; post village in Chickasaw Nation on Chicago, Rock
 Island and Pacific Railway; elevation, 847 feet .... Addington.
Sulphur; branch in Choctaw and Chickasaw nations, a right-
 hand branch of Sandy Creek, a tributary to Clear Boggy
 Creek .... Atoka.
Sulphur; creek in Cherokee Nation, a right-hand branch of
 Neosho River .... Pryor.
Sulphur; creek in Chickasaw Nation, a left-hand branch of
 Rock Creek, a tributary to Washita River .... Stonewall.
Sulphur; creek in Choctaw Nation, a left-hand branch of
 Muddy Boggy Creek .... Coalgate.
Sulphur Creek; village in Chickasaw Nation .... Stonewall.
Sulphur Springs or Sulphur; town in Chickasaw Nation
 on St. Louis and San Francisco Railroad; population, 1,198. Stonewall.
Summerfield; creek in Cherokee Nation, a left-hand branch
 of Neosho River .... Siloam Springs.
Summerfield; post village in Choctaw Nation .... Winding Stair.
Summit; post village in Creek Nation on Missouri, Kansas,
 and Texas Railway; elevation, 595 feet .... Muscogee.
Surprise; creek in Choctaw Nation, a right-hand branch of
 Mountain Fork River, a tributary to Little River .... Lukfata.
Sutter; post village in Choctaw Nation.
Swink; post village in Choctaw Nation.
Sycamore; creek in Chickasaw Nation, a left-hand branch of
 Washita River .... Tishomingo.
Sycamore; creek in Choctaw Nation, a left-hand branch of
 Kiamichi River .... Winding Stair.
Sylvan; post village in Chickasaw Nation .... Tishomingo.
Tahlequah; capital of Cherokee Nation on St. Louis and San
 Francisco Railroad; population, 1,482................... Tahlequah.
Tahlequah; creek in Cherokee Nation, a right-hand branch of
 Illinois River .... Tahlequah.
Tahlequah Hollow; valley of Tahlequah Creek, a tributary
 to Arkansas River, in Cherokee Nation .... Siloam Springs.
Talala; creek in Cherokee Nation, a right-hand branch of Ver-
 digris River, heading in North and South forks........... Nowata.
Talala; post village in Cherokee Nation on St. Louis, Iron
 Mountain and Southern Railway; elevation, 683 feet...... Nowata.
Talihina; post village in Choctaw Nation on St. Louis and San
 Francisco Railroad .... Tuskahoma.
Taloka; creek in Choctaw Nation, a small right-hand branch
 of Canadian River.................................... Sansbois.
Tamaha; post village in Choctaw Nation on the Arkansas River;
 population, 237...................................... Sallisaw.
Tanaha; station on St. Louis and San Francisco Railroad.

Tandy; village in Choctaw Nation on Choctaw, Oklahoma and
Gulf Railroad .... Coalgate.
Tanner; creek in Choctaw Nation, a right-hand branch of
North Boggy Creek, a tributary to Muddy Boggy Creek... Claremore.
Tanyard; creek in Choctaw Nation, a left-hand branch of
Muddy Boggy Creek .... Antlers.
Tate; post village in Seminole Nation.
Tate Parris; branch in Cherokee Nation, a left-hand branch
of Illinois River, a tributary to Arkansas River........... Siloam Springs.
Tatums; post village in Chickasaw Nation.
Taylor; ferry across Neosho River in Cherokee Nation .... Muscogee.
Teeler; post village in Chickasaw Nation on Choctaw, Okla-
homa and Gulf Railroad .... Tishomingo.
Tellico; station on Missouri, Kansas and Texas Railway.
Tenmile; creek in Choctaw Nation, a right-hand branch of
Kiamichi River, heading in South Fork and Tenmile
creeks .... Antlers.
Terral; post village in Chickasaw Nation on Chicago, Rock
Island and Pacific Railway; elevation, 843 feet............ Montague.
Terrapin; creek in Cherokee Nation, a left-hand branch of
Illinois River .... Tahlequah.
Terrapin; creek in Choctaw Nation, a left-hand branch of
Little River... Alikchi.
Texanna; post village in Cherokee Nation .... Sansbois.
Thackerville; post village in Chickasaw Nation on Gulf, Colo-
rado and Santa Fe Railway; population, 154; elevation, 862
feet.. Ardmore.
The Cut Off; part of Poteau River in Choctaw Nation cut off·
by the course of the river being changed.................. Sallisaw.
The Narrows; gap in the Pine Mountains in Choctaw Nation
through which Mountain Fork River flows................. Lukfata.
The Twins; summits in Creek Nation......................... Okmulgee.
Thomasville; post village in Choctaw Nation on Kansas City
Southern Railway .... Winding Stair.
Thompson; creek in Cherokee Nation, a right-hand branch of
Pawpaw Creek, a tributary to Neosho River, through Cabin
Creek.. Vinita.
Threemile Creek; branch in Chickasaw Nation, a left-hand
branch of Mill Creek, a tributary to Washita River....... Tishomingo.
Thurman; village in Choctaw Nation .... Canadian.
Ti; post village in Choctaw Nation.
Tiawah; post village in Cherokee Nation on St. Louis, Iron
Mountain and Southern Railway; elevation, 610 feet.
Tidmore; post village in Seminole Nation on Choctaw, Okla-
homa and Gulf Railroad.
Tiger; creek in Creek Nation, a right-hand branch of Wewoka
Creek, a tributary to North Fork of Canadian River ...... Wewoka.
Tiger; creek in Seminole Nation, a left-hand branch of We-
woka Creek, a tributary to North Fork of Canadian River. Seminole.
Timber; post village in Creek Nation.
Timberlake; creek in Cherokee Nation, a left-hand branch of
Caney River, a tributary to Verdigris River.............. Nowata.
Timberland; post village in Cherokee Nation.
Timberley; creek in Creek and Cherokee nations, a right-hand
branch of Dirty Creek, a tributary to Arkansas River..... Muscogee.

Tishomingo; capital of Chickasaw Nation on Choctaw, Oklahoma and Gulf Railroad .... Tishomingo.

Tomike; creek in Chickasaw Nation, a right-hand branch of Canadian River .... Pauls Valley.

Troy; post village in Chickasaw Nation on St. Louis and San Francisco Railroad.

Truax; post village in Chickasaw Nation.

Tucker; creek in Cherokee Nation, a left-hand branch of Verdigris River, a tributary to Arkansas River. { Nowata. / Vinita.

Tucker; post village in Choctaw Nation .... Sallisaw.

Tucker Knob; summit in Choctaw Nation................... Sansbois.

Tulip; creek in Chickasaw Nation, a left-hand branch of Caddo Creek .... Ardmore.

Tullahassee; post village in Creek Nation.................... Muscogee.

Tulsa; post village in Creek Nation on St. Louis and San Francisco Railroad; population, 1,390; elevation, 700 feet. Claremore.

Turkey; branch in Choctaw Nation, a right-hand branch of Cedar Creek, a tributary to Kiamichi..................... { Alikchi. / Antlers.

Turkey; creek in Chickasaw Nation, a right-hand branch of Washita River .... Tishomingo.

Turkey; creek in Choctaw Nation, a right-hand branch of Sansbois Creek, a tributary to Arkansas River............. Sansbois.

Turkey; creek in Choctaw Nation, a right-hand branch of Little River. { Antlers. / Alikchi.

Turkey; creek in Choctaw Nation, a right-hand branch of Mountain Fork River, a tributary to Little River......... Lukfata.

Turkey; creek in Creek Nation, a left-hand branch of Little Deep Fork Creek, a tributary to Deep Fork Canadian River. Nuyaka.

Turkey; creek in Seminole Nation, a right-hand branch of North Fork of Canadian River........................... Seminole.

Turkey; spring in Chickasaw Nation......................... Tishomingo.

Turkey Sandy; creek in Chickasaw Nation, a right-hand branch of Kickapoo Sandy Creek, a tributary to Washita River... Pauls Valley.

Turkey Snout Ridge; summit in the Blue Bouncer Mountains in Choctaw Nation, a part of the Kiamichi Mountains. Winding Stair.

Turley; post village in Cherokee Nation .... Claremore.

Turner; post village in Creek Nation.

Tuskahoma; post village in Choctaw Nation on St. Louis and San Francisco Railroad .... Tuskahoma.

Tuskegee; post village in Creek Nation..................... Nuyaka.

Tussy; post village in Chickasaw Nation.

Tuttle; post village in Chickasaw Nation on St. Louis and San Francisco Railroad.

Twin; crescent-shaped lake in the bottom lands of Red River, in Choctaw Nation .... Shawneetown.

Twine; post village in Creek Nation.

Tyler; branch in Cherokee Nation, a left-hand branch of Cabin Creek, a tributary to Neosho River...................... Vinita.

Tyler; post village in Chickasaw Nation.

Tyner; creek in Cherokee Nation, a right-hand branch of Barren Creek, a tributary to Illinois River. { Tahlequah. / Siloam Springs.

Tyrola; post village in Chickasaw Nation.................... Stonewall.

Ulm; village in Cherokee Nation............................ Siloam Springs.

Ulm Prairie; level stretch of land in Cherokee Nation near the village of Ulm.. Siloam Springs.

Umbria; village in Chickasaw Nation on Gulf, Colorado and Santa Fe Railway .... Ardmore.

Uphill; creek in Choctaw Nation, a small left-hand branch of Wildhorse Creek, a tributary to Little River .... Tuskahoma.

Upson; station on St. Louis, Iron Mountain and Southern Railway.

Utica; post village in Choctaw Nation.

Valley; station on Missouri, Kansas and Texas Railway.

Valliant; post village in Choctaw Nation on St. Louis and San Francisco Railroad.

Vance; post village in Creek Nation.

Vann; a small village in Cherokee Nation .... Sansbois.

Vaughn; village in Chickasaw Nation........................ Tishomingo.

Velma; post village in Chickasaw Nation.................... Addington.

Vera; station on Atchison, Topeka and Santa Fe Railway.

Verdigris; village in Cherokee Nation on St. Louis and San Francisco Railroad; elevation 608 feet .... Claremore.

Verdigris; river of Kansas and Indian Territory. A large left-hand branch of Arkansas River heading in southeast Kansas and flowing with a general southward course through the northern part of Indian Territory to its mouth. The mouth is half a mile above that of the Neosho River and indications are that in former times the Verdigris joined the Neosho River just above the mouth of the latter in the bottom lands of the Arkansas. Its length is 275 miles. It is in Creek and Cherokee nations. } Nowata. Claremore. Okmulgee. Muscogee.

Vian; creek in Cherokee Nation; a left-hand branch of Arkansas River. } Sallisaw. Tahlequah.

Vian; post village in Cherokee Nation on St. Louis, Iron Mountain and Southern Railway; population, 296; elevation, 546 feet .... Sallisaw.

Victor; lake in Choctaw Nation .... Shawneetown.

Victor; post village in Choctaw Nation.

Victor; village in Chickasaw Nation .... Stonewall.

Vinegar; creek in Cherokeee Nation, a small right-hand branch of Verdigris River, a tributary to Arkansas River.. Nowata.

Vinita; town in Cherokee Nation on Missouri, Kansas and Texas Railway; population, 2,339; elevation, 695 feet..... Vinita.

Viola; post village in Chickasaw Nation..................... Tishomingo.

Vireton; post village in Choctaw Nation.

Wade; post village in Choctaw Nation .... Bonham.

Wadena; station on St. Louis and San Francisco Railroad; elevation, 490 feet.

Wagoner; town in Creek Nation on St. Louis and San Francisco and Missouri, Kansas and Texas railroads; population, 2,372; elevation, 578 feet .... Muscogee.

Waldon; post village in Chickasaw Nation .... Chickasha.

Walker; post village in Chickasaw Nation .... Pauls Valley.

Walkingstick Hollow; valley of Walkingstick Creek, a right-hand branch of Sallisaw Creek, a tributary to Arkansas River, in Cherokee Nation .... Tahlequah.

Walkingstick Mountain; summit in Cherokee Nation...... Tahlequah.

Walls; post village in Choctaw Nation .... Sallisaw.

Wallville; post village in Chickasaw Nation.................. Rush Springs.

Walnut; creek in Chickasaw Nation, a left-hand branch of {Ardmore.
Red River, known in its lower course as Walnut Bayou. {Addington.

Walnut; creek in Chicasaw Nation, a right-hand branch of {Chickasha.
Canadian River, heading in North Fork.   {Purcell.

Walnut; creek in Choctaw Nation, a left-hand branch of Kiamichi River... Tuskahoma.

Walnut; creek in Creek Nation, a right-hand branch of Cane
Creek, a tributary to Arkansas River .... Okmulgee.

Walnut; group of hills in Choctaw Nation south of Kiamichi
River.. Winding Stair.

Walnut; small mountain ridge in Choctaw Nation, a part of
Kiamichi Mountains .... Winding Stair.

Walnut; post village in Cherokee Nation.

Wanette; station on Gulf, Colorado and Santa Fe Railway.

Wanhillan; village in Cherokee Nation...................... Tahlequah.

Wann; post village in Cherokee Nation on Missouri, Kansas
and Texas Railway.

Wapanucka; creek in Chickasaw Nation, a right-hand branch {Atoka.
of Delaware Creek, a tributary to Clear Boggy Creek.   {Tishomingo.

Wapanucka; post village in Choctaw Nation on Choctaw,
Oklahoma and Gulf Railroad............................. Atoka.

Ward; post village in Choctaw Nation .... Sallisaw.

Wards; creek in Choctaw Nation, a left-hand branch of North {Claremore.
Boggy Creek, a tributary to Muddy Boggy Creek.   {McAlester.

Warner; creek in Creek Nation, a left-hand branch of Polecat
Creek, a tributary to Arkansas River .... Nuyaka.

Washington; creek in Chickasaw Nation, a left-hand branch
of Washita River.. Pauls Valley.

Washington Ranch; a village in Chickasaw Nation .... Gainesville.

Washita; river, a large left-hand branch of Red River heading {Rush Springs.
in the central part of Oklahoma Territory, and after a long {Pauls Valley.
course, generally toward the southeast but ranging from {Ardmore.
south to east, entering Red River in Chickasaw Nation. {Tishomingo.
{Denison.

Washita; village in Chickasaw Nation; elevation, 809 feet.... Pauls Valley.

Wasseta; station on Missouri, Kansas and Texas Railway.

Wasson; post village in Cherokee Nation on Missouri, Kansas
and Texas Railway....................................... Vinita.

Waterfall; slough in Choctaw Nation, a back-water from Mintubbe Lake .... Shawneetown.

Waterhole; creek in Choctaw Nation, a right-hand branch of
Perry Creek, a tributary to Red River .... Shawneetown.

Watonville; village in Creek Nation........................ Wewoka.

Watova; post village in Cherokee Nation on St. Louis, Iron
Mountain and Southern Railway; elevation, 720 feet ..... Nowata.

Watson; ferry across Red River in Choctaw Nation.......... Shawneetown.

Wauhillan; post village in Cherokee Nation.

Wayne; post village in Chickasaw Nation on Gulf, Colorado
and Santa Fe Railroad; elevation, 1,100 feet.............. Pauls Valley.

Wealaka; post village in Creek Nation...................... Okmulgee.

Weaverton; post village in Chickasaw Nation................ Tishomingo.

Webb; creek in Chickasaw Nation, a left-hand branch of Red
 River.. Bonham.

Webbers Falls; post village in Cherokee Nation; population,
 211.. Muscogee.

Weer; post village in Creek Nation........................... Okmulgee.

Weetwater Hollow; valley of Weetwater Creek, a tributary
 to Neosho River, in Cherokee Nation .... Wyandotte.

Welch; post village in Cherokee Nation on Missouri, Kansas
 and Texas Railway; population, 334; elevation, 825 feet.. Vinita.

Welch Mountain; summit in Cherokee Nation.............. Tahlequah.

Weldon; post village in Cherokee Nation.

Weleetka; post village in Creek Nation.

Welling; post village in Cherokee Nation.

Wellington (Lee post-office); village in Creek Nation........ Okmulgee.

Wells; station on Missouri, Kansas and Texas Railway.

Wesley; post village in Choctaw Nation.

West; fork in Choctaw Nation, a right-hand branch of Glover
 Creek, a tributary to Little River......................... Lukfata.

West; fork of Cabin Creek, a tributary to Neosho River, in
 Cherokee Nation .... Vinita.

West Cedar; creek in Cherokee Nation, a fork of Skin Bayou
 Creek, a tributary to Arkansas River .... Tahlequah.

West Eagletown; village in Choctaw Nation .... Lukfata.

Western; branch in Cherokee Nation, a right-hand branch of
 Verdigris River, a tributary to Arkansas River .... Nowata.

West Muskogee; station on St. Louis and San Francisco Railroad.

Westville; post village in Cherokee Nation on Kansas City
 Southern Railway; population, 296 .... Tahlequah.

Wet Prairie; level stretch of land in the northeast part of
 Cherokee Nation .... Siloam Springs.

Wetumka; post village in Creek Nation..................... Wewoka.

Wewoka; capital of Seminole Nation on Choctaw, Oklahoma
 and Gulf Railroad .... Wewoka.

Wewoka; creek in Creek and Seminole nations, a right-hand ⎰Wewoka.
 branch of North Fork of Canadian River.   ⎱Seminole.

Wheeler; post village in Chickasaw Nation.................. Ardmore.

Whiskey; branch in Cherokee Nation, a left-hand branch of
 Cabin Creek, a tributary to Neosho River................. Vinita.

Whiskey; creek in Chickasaw Nation, a right-hand branch of
 Walnut Creek, a tributary to Red River................... Gainesville.

Whiskey; creek in Chickasaw Nation, a small intermittent
 right-hand branch of Wildhorse Creek, a tributary to
 Washita River .... Pauls Valley.

Whiskey; ford across Neosho River in Cherokee Nation ..... Muscogee.

Whitebread; post village in Chickasaw Nation.............. Pauls Valley.

White; creek in Cherokee Nation, a right-hand branch of Pawpaw Creek, a tributary to Neosho River, through Cabin
 Creek .... Vinita.

Whitefield; post village in Choctaw Nation .... Tahlequah.

Whitegrass; creek in Chickasaw Nation, a left-hand branch
 of Red River .... Paris.

White Grass; creek in Choctaw Nation, a left-hand branch of
 Red River .... Shawneetown.

Whitmire; post village in Cherokee Nation .... Siloam Springs.
Whiteoak; creek in Cherokee Nation, a right-hand branch of
Cedar Creek, a tributary to Neosho River................ Vinita.
Whiteoak; post village in Cherokee Nation on St. Louis and
San Francisco Railroad; elevation, 765 feet .... Vinita.
Whitewater; creek in Cherokee Nation, a left-hand branch of {Siloam Springs.
Neosho River.   {Wyandotte.
Widow Moore; creek in Chickasaw Nation, a left-hand branch
of Washita River.. Tishomingo.
Wilburton; post village in Choctaw Nation, on Choctaw,
Oklahoma and Gulf Railroad; elevation, 652 feet......... Tuskahoma.
                                                          ⎧Pauls Valley.
Wildhorse; creek in Chickasha Nation, a right-hand branch of⎪Ardmore.
Washita River.   ⎨Addington.
                                                          ⎩Rush Springs.
Wildhorse; creek in Choctaw Nation, a right-hand branch of⎧McAlester.
Coal Creek, a tributary to Canadian River, through Gaines⎨Canadian.
Creek.
Wildhorse; creek in Choctaw Nation, a right-hand branch of
Brazil Creek, a tributary to Poteau River .... Sallisaw.
Wildhorse; creek in Choctaw Nation, a left-hand branch of
Little River.. Tuskahoma.
Wildhorse; small mountain ridge in Cherokee Nation, a part
of Kiamichi Mountain .... Sallisaw.
Wiley; post village in Chickasaw Nation .... Tishomingo.
Williams; mountain in Choctaw Nation, a part of Pine Moun-
tains .... Lukfata.
Willis; ferry across Red River in Chickasaw Nation.......... Denison.
Willis; ferry across Little River in Choctaw Nation .... Shawneetown.
Willis; post village in Chickasaw Nation .... Denison.
Willow; branch in Chickasaw Nation, a right-hand branch of
Mud Creek, a tributary to Red River .... Addington.
Willow Sandy; creek in Chickasaw Nation, a left-hand branch
of Cherokee Sandy Creek, a tributary to Washita River.. Pauls Valley.
Wilson; post village in Chickasaw Nation.................... Ardmore.
                                                          ⎧Ardmore.
Wilson; creek in Chickasaw Nation, a left-hand branch of⎨Denison.
Red River.   ⎩Tishomingo.
Wilson; summit in Rich Mountains in Choctaw Nation ...... Winding Stair.
Wimer; post village in Cherokee Nation.
Winding Stair Mountain; broken, irregular ridge of the⎤Poteau Mountain.
Ozark Hills, lying north of the valley of Kiamichi River,⎥Winding Stair.
in Choctaw Nation, with a maximum altitude of 2,550 ⎥Tuskahoma.
feet.   ⎦
Winter; creek in Chickasaw Nation, a left-hand branch of
Washita River, heading in East and West Winter creeks.. Rush Springs.
Winthrop; station on Atchison, Topeka and Santa Fe Railway.
Wister; post village in Choctaw Nation on Choctaw, Okla-
homa and Gulf and St. Louis and San Francisco railroads;
population, 313; elevation, 478 feet...................... Winding Stair.
Witteville; post village in Choctaw Nation.................. Sallisaw.
Womack; post village in Chickasaw Nation.
Wolf; creek in Cherokee Nation, a right-hand branch of
Neosho River .... Pryor.

Wolf; creek in Chickasaw Nation, a left-hand branch of
Washita River .... Pauls Valley.
Wolf; creek in Choctaw Nation, a left-hand branch of Little {Lukfata.
River.   {Alikchi.
Wolf; creek in Choctaw Nation, a left-hand branch of Brazil
Creek, a tributary to Poteau River....................... Sallisaw.
Wolf; creek in Choctaw Nation, a left-hand branch of Island
Bayou, a tributary to Red River.......................... Bonham.
Wolf; creek in Creek Nation, a right-hand branch of Salt {Wewoka.
Creek, a tributary to Deep Fork of Canadian River.   {Nuyaka.
Wolf; creek in Creek Nation, a left-hand branch of Deep Fork
of Canadian River, a tributary to North Fork of Canadian
River... Canadian.
Wolf; mountain, a summit in Choctaw Nation............... Sallisaw.
Wolf; post village in Seminole Nation.
Wolse; creek in Cherokee Nation, a right-hand branch of Ver-
digris River, heading in North and South forks........... Nowata.
Woodford; post village in Chickasaw Nation .... Ardmore.
Woodley; post village in Cherokee Nation .... Vinita.
Woods Spring; branch in Cherokee Nation, a right-hand {Siloam Springs.
branch of Drowning Creek, a tributary to Neosho River.   {Wyandotte.
Woodville; post village in Chickasaw Nation on St. Louis and
San Francisco Railroad.................................... Denison.
Woodward Hollow; valley of Woodward Creek, a tributary
to Neosho River, in Cherokee Nation .... Wyandotte.
Woolsey; post village in Chickasaw Nation................... Addington.
Worley; creek in Chickasaw Nation, a right-hand branch of
Canadian River .... Chickasha.
Wyandotte; post village in Cherokee Nation; population, 224. Wyandotte.
Wyandotte; reservation in the northeastern part of the Ter-
ritory with an area of 33 square miles. Population, 1,213;
992 white and 221 Indian .... Wyandotte.
Wyatt; post village in Chickasaw Nation................... Tishomingo.
Wybark; post village in Creek Nation on Missouri, Kansas and
Texas Railway.. Muscogee.
Wynnewood; post village in Chickasaw Nation on Gulf, Colo-
rado and Santa Fe Railway; population, 1,907; elevation,
857 feet... Pauls Valley.
Yanubbe; creek in Choctaw Nation, a left-hand branch of {Lukfata.
Little River.   {Shawneetown.
Yarnaby; creek in Chickasaw Nation, a left-hand branch of
Red River.. Bonham.
Yarnaby; post village in Chickasaw Nation.................. Bonham.
Yarrow; post village in Creek Nation...................... Nuyaka.
Yashoo; creek in Choctaw Nation, a left-hand branch of Little {Lukfata.
River.   {Shawneetown.
Yeager; post village in Creek Nation on St. Louis and San
Francisco Railroad.
Yellow Water; creek in Creek Nation, a left-hand branch of
Arkansas River .... Okmulgee.
Yhola; branch in Creek Nation, a left-hand branch of Nuyaka
Creek, a tributary to Deep Fork of Canadian River....... Nuyaka.
York; post village in Chickasaw Nation..................... Stonewall.
Yuba; post village in Chickasaw Nation.
Zena; post village in Cherokee Nation .... Siloam Springs.

O

PUBLICATIONS OF UNITED STATES GEOLOGICAL SURVEY.

[Bulletin No. 248.]

The publications of the United States Geological Survey consist of (1) Annual Reports, (2) Monographs, (3) Professional Papers, (4) Bulletins, (5) Mineral Resources, (6) Water-Supply and Irrigation Papers, (7) Topographic Atlas of United States—folios and separate sheets thereof, (8) Geologic Atlas of United States—folios thereof. The classes numbered 2, 7, and 8 are sold at cost of publication; the others are distributed free. A circular giving complete lists may be had on application.

The Professional Papers, Bulletins, and Water-Supply Papers treat of a variety of subjects, and the total number issued is large. They have therefore been classified into the following series: A, Economic geology; B, Descriptive geology; C, Systematic geology and paleontology; D, Petrography and mineralogy; E, Chemistry and physics; F, Geography; G, Miscellaneous; H, Forestry; I, Irrigation; J, Water storage; K, Pumping water; L, Quality of water; M, General hydrographic investigations; N, Water power; O, Underground waters; P, Hydrographic progress reports. This bulletin is the forty-fourth in Series F, the complete list of which follows (all are bulletins thus far):

SERIES F, GEOGRAPHY.

5. Dictionary of altitudes in United States, by Henry Gannett. 1884. 325 pp. (Out of stock; see Bulletin 160.)
6. Elevations in Dominion of Canada, by J. W. Spencer. 1884. 43 pp. (Out of stock.)
13. Boundaries of United States and of the several States and Territories, with historical sketch of territorial changes, by Henry Gannett. 1885. 135 pp. (Out of stock; see Bulletin 171.)
48. On form and position of sea level, by R. S. Woodward. 1888. 88 pp. (Out of stock.)
49. Latitudes and longitudes of certain points in Missouri, Kansas, and New Mexico, by R. S. Woodward. 1889. 133 pp.
50. Formulas and tables to facilitate the construction and use of maps, by R. S. Woodward. 1889. 124 pp. (Out of stock.)
70. Report on astronomical work of 1889 and 1890, by R. S. Woodward. 1890. 79 pp.
72. Altitudes between Lake Superior and Rocky Mountains, by Warren Upham. 1891. 229 pp.
76. Dictionary of altitudes in United States (second edition), by Henry Gannett. 1891. 393 pp. (Out of stock; see Bulletin 160.)
115. Geographic dictionary of Rhode Island, by Henry Gannett. 1894. 31 pp.
116. Geographic dictionary of Massachusetts, by Henry Gannett. 1894. 126 pp.
117. Geographic dictionary of Connecticut, by Henry Gannett. 1894. 67 pp.
118. Geographic dictionary of New Jersey, by Henry Gannett. 1894. 131 pp.
122. Results of primary triangulation, by Henry Gannett. 1894. 412 pp., 17 pls. (Out of stock.)
123. Dictionary of geographic positions, by Henry Gannett. 1895. 183 pp., 1 map. (Out of stock.)
154. Gazetteer of Kansas, by Henry Gannett. 1898. 246 pp., 6 pls.
160. Dictionary of altitudes in United States (third edition), by Henry Gannett. 1899. 775 pp. (Out of stock.)
166. Gazetteer of Utah, by Henry Gannett. 1900. 43 pp., 1 map.
169. Altitudes in Alaska, by Henry Gannett. 1900. 13 pp.
170. Survey of boundary line between Idaho and Montana from international boundary to crest of Bitterroot Mountains, by R. U. Goode. 1900. 67 pp., 14 pls.
171. Boundaries of United States and of the several States and Territories, with outline of history of all important changes of territory (second edition), by Henry Gannett. 1900. 142 pp., 53 pls. (Out of stock.)
174. Survey of northwestern boundary of United States, 1857-1861, by Marcus Baker. 1900. 78 pp., 1 pl.
175. Triangulation and spirit leveling in Indian Territory, by C. H. Fitch. 1900. 141 pp., 1 pl.
181. Results of primary triangulation and primary traverse, fiscal year 1900-1901, by H. M. Wilson, J. H. Renshawe, E. M. Douglas, and R. U. Goode. 1901. 240 pp., 1 map.
183. Gazetteer of Porto Rico, by Henry Gannett. 1901. 51 pp.

185. Results of spirit leveling, fiscal year 1900-1901, by H. M. Wilson, J. H. Renshawe, E. M. Douglas, and R. U. Goode. 1901. 219 pp.
187. Geographic dictionary of Alaska, by Marcus Baker. 1901. 443 pp. (Out of stock.)
190. Gazetteer of Texas, by Henry Gannett. 1902. 162 pp., 8 pls. (Out of stock.)
192. Gazetteer of Cuba, by Henry Gannett. 1902. 113 pp., 8 pls. (Out of stock.)
194. Northwest boundary of Texas, by Marcus Baker. 1902. 51 pp., 1 pl.
196. Topographic development of the Klamath Mountains, by J. S. Diller. 1902. 69 pp., 13 pls.
197. The origin of certain place names in the United States, by Henry Gannett. 1902. 280 pp. (Out of stock.)
201. Results of primary triangulation and primary traverse, fiscal year 1901-2, by H. M. Wilson, J. H. Renshawe, E. M. Douglas, and R. U. Goode. 1902. 164 pp., 1 pl.
214. Geographic tables and formulas, compiled by S. S. Gannett. 1903. 284 pp.
216. Results of primary triangulation and primary traverse, fiscal year 1902-3, by S. S. Gannett. 1903. 222 pp., 1 pl.
224. Gazetteer of Texas (second edition), by Henry Gannett. 1904. 177 pp., 7 pls.
226. Boundaries of the United States and of the several States and Territories, with an outline of the history of all important changes of territory (third edition), by Henry Gannett. 1904. 145 pp., 54 pls.
230. Gazetteer of Delaware, by Henry Gannett. 1904. 15 pp.
231. Gazetteer of Maryland, by Henry Gannett. 1904. 84 pp.
232. Gazetteer of Virginia, by Henry Gannett. 1904. 159 pp.
233. Gazetteer of West Virginia, by Henry Gannett. 1904. 164 pp.
234. Geographic tables and formulas (second edition), compiled by S. S. Gannett. 1904. 310 pp.
245. Results of primary triangulation and primary traverse, fiscal year 1902-3, by S. S. Gannett. 1904. — pp., 1 pl.
248. Gazetter of Indian Territory, by Henry Gannett. 1904. 70 pp.

Correspondence should be addressed to

The DIRECTOR,

UNITED STATES GEOLOGICAL SURVEY,

WASHINGTON, D. C.

DECEMBER, 1904.

Author.

Gannett, Henry, 1846–

. . . A gazetteer of Indian Territory, by Henry Gannett. Washington, Gov't Print. off., 1905.

70, iii p. 23½ᶜᵐ. (U. S. Geological survey. Bulletin no. 248.)
Subject series: F, Geography, 44.

1. Indian Territory—Descr. & trav.—Gazetteers.

Subject.

Gannett, Henry, 1846–

. . . A gazetteer of Indian Territory, by Henry Gannett. Washington, Gov't print. off., 1905.

70, iii p. 23½ᶜᵐ. (U. S. Geological survey. Bulletin no. 248.)
Subject series: F, Geography, 44.

1. Indian Territory—Descr. & trav.—Gazetteers.

Series.

U. S. Geological survey.

Bulletins.

no. 248. Gannett, Henry. A gazetteer of Indian Territory. 1905.

Reference.

U. S. Dept. of the Interior.

see also

U. S. Geological survey.

Bull. 248—04——6

www.ingramcontent.com/pod-product-compliance
Lightning Source LLC
Chambersburg PA
CBHW031006090426
42737CB00008B/696